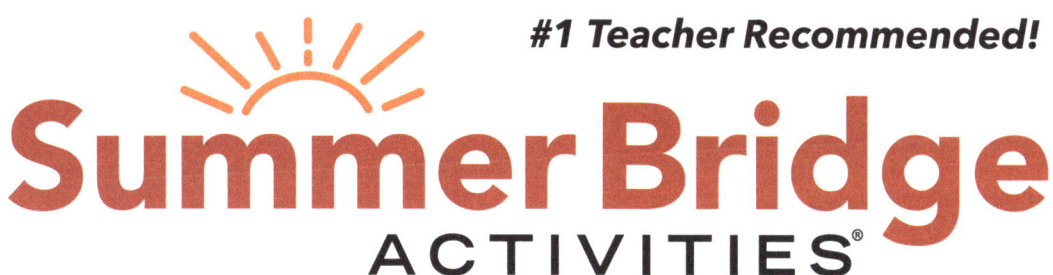

#1 Teacher Recommended!

BRIDGING GRADES
7 to 8

Carson Dellosa Education
Greensboro, North Carolina

Caution: Exercise activities may require adult supervision. Before beginning any exercise activity, consult a physician. Written parental permission is suggested for those using this book in group situations. Children should always warm up prior to beginning any exercise activity and should stop immediately if they feel any discomfort during exercise.

Caution: Before beginning any food activity, ask parents' permission and inquire about the child's food allergies and religious or other food restrictions.

Caution: Nature activities may require adult supervision. Before beginning any nature activity, ask parents' permission and inquire about the child's plant and animal allergies. Remind the child not to touch plants or animals during the activity without adult supervision.

Caution: Before completing any balloon activity, ask parents' permission and inquire about possible latex allergies. Also, remember that uninflated or popped balloons may present a choking hazard.

The authors and publisher are not responsible or liable for any injury that may result from performing the exercises or activities in this book.

Summer Bridge®
An imprint of Carson Dellosa Education
PO Box 35665
Greensboro, NC 27425 USA

© 2015 Carson Dellosa Education. Except as permitted under the United States Copyright Act, no part of this publication may be reproduced, stored, or distributed in any form or by any means (mechanically, electronically, recording, etc.) without the prior written consent of Carson Dellosa Education.

Printed in the USA • All rights reserved.

ISBN 978-1-4838-1587-9

01-1662412735

Table of Contents

Making the Most of *Summer Bridge Activities*®..iv
Skills Matrix vi
Summer Reading for Everyone viii
Summer Learning Is Everywhere! x

Section I: Monthly Goals and Word List 1
Introduction to Flexibility 2
Activity Pages 3
Science Experiments 43
Social Studies Activities 45
Outdoor Extension Activities 48

Section II: Monthly Goals and Word List 49
Introduction to Strength 50
Activity Pages 51
Science Experiments 91
Social Studies Activities 93
Outdoor Extension Activities 96

Section III: Monthly Goals and Word List 97
Introduction to Endurance 98
Activity Pages 99
Science Experiments 139
Social Studies Activities 141
Outdoor Extension Activities 144

Answer Key..145
Flash Cards
Certificate of Completion

Making the Most of *Summer Bridge Activities*®

This book will help your child review seventh grade skills and preview eighth grade skills. Inside, find lots of resources that encourage your child to practice, learn, and grow while getting a head start on the new school year ahead.

Just 15 Minutes a Day

...is all it takes to stay sharp with learning activities for each weekday, all summer long!

Month-by-Month Organization

Three color-coded sections match the three months of summer vacation. Each month begins with a goal-setting and vocabulary-building activity. You'll also find an introduction to the section's fitness and character-building focus.

Daily Activities

Two pages of activities are provided for each weekday. They'll take about 15 minutes to complete. Activities will help your child practice these skills and more:

- Grammar and usage
- Writing
- Reading comprehension
- Vocabulary
- Algebraic equations
- Working with exponents
- Geometry
- Statistics and probability

Plenty of Bonus Features
...match your child's needs and interests!

Bonus Activities

Social studies activities explore places, maps, and more—a perfect complement to summer travel. Science experiments invite your child to interact with the world and build critical thinking skills.

Take It Outside!

A collection of fun ideas for outdoor observation, exploration, learning, and play is provided for each summer month.

Special Features

FITNESS FLASH: Quick exercises to develop strength, flexibility, and fitness

CHARACTER CHECK: Ideas for developing kindness, honesty, tolerance, and more

FACTOID: Fun trivia facts

Skill-Building Flash Cards

Cut out the cards at the back of the book. Store in a zip-top bag or punch a hole in each one and thread on a ring. Take the cards along with you for practice on the go.

Certificate of Congratulations

At the end of the summer, complete and present the certificate at the back of the book. Congratulate your child for being well prepared for the next school year.

Skills Matrix

Day	Algebra & Ratios	Character Development	Critical Thinking	Data Analysis & Probability	Decimals, Fractions & Percentages	Fitness	Geometry & Measurement	Grammar	Language Arts	Literary Terms	Multiplication & Division	Parts of Speech	Problem Solving	Reading Comprehension	Science	Social Studies	Vocabulary	Writing
1							★	★							★		★	
2							★		★					★			★	
3	★													★			★	
4	★																★	★
5				★		★	★										★	
6				★				★						★				
7			★				★	★									★	
8				★			★			★								
9				★			★							★				
10		★		★				★									★	
11							★		★				★			★		
12										★		★	★					★
13	★						★		★									
14	★											★		★				★
15	★					★				★		★						
16												★		★			★	
17					★			★			★					★		
18	★						★	★							★			
19											★	★		★				
20								★	★				★					★
				★				BONUS PAGES!							★	★		★
1	★						★								★		★	
2	★												★	★				
3	★																★	
4						★		★									★	★
5							★	★						★				
6							★		★								★	★
7	★		★	★														
8							★					★	★					
9			★			★							★				★	
10							★						★		★		★	
11	★								★					★				

Skills Matrix

Day	Algebra & Ratios	Character Development	Critical Thinking	Data Analysis & Probability	Decimals, Fractions, & Percentages	Fitness	Geometry & Measurement	Grammar	Language Arts	Literary Terms	Multiplication & Division	Parts of Speech	Problem Solving	Reading Comprehension	Science	Social Studies	Vocabulary	Writing
12							★					★		★				
13						★		★			★							★
14	★							★						★				
15	★								★			★			★			
16							★							★		★	★	
17							★							★				
18							★			★				★	★			
19				★			★		★									★
20	★													★				
Bonus						★	BONUS	PAGES! ★							★	★		★
1							★	★			★						★	
2	★						★										★	★
3												★	★	★				
4	★					★			★						★			
5	★								★			★			★			
6							★	★						★				
7	★													★		★	★	
8	★															★	★	
9							★	★						★				
10							★	★		★				★				
11							★							★				★
12							★						★	★				
13	★	★							★					★				
14				★						★				★				
15							★							★			★	
16				★					★					★	★			
17						★	★		★									★
18	★								★					★				
19						★		★	★								★	
20			★				★						★			★		
Bonus				★	★		BONUS	PAGES!							★	★		

Summer Reading for Everyone

Reading is the single most important skill for school success. Experts recommend that seventh and eighth grade students read for at least 30 minutes each day. Help your child choose several books from this list based on his or her interests. Choose at least one fiction (F) and one nonfiction (NF) title. Then, head to the local library to begin your reading adventure!

If you like comic books and graphic novels...
Nimona
    by Noelle Stevenson (F)
American Born Chinese
    by Gene Luen Yang (NF)

If you like science fiction...
The Hitchhiker's Guide to the Galaxy
    by Douglas Adams (F)
The Giver
    by Lois Lowry (F)

If you like history...
Echo
    by Pam Muñoz Ryan (F)
The Endless Steppe
    by Esther Hautzig (NF)

If you like mysteries...
The Art of Secrets
    by James Klise (F)
Killer Lipstick and Other Spy Gadgets
    by Don Rauf (NF)

© Carson Dellosa Education

If you like animals...
Summer of the Monkeys
  by Wilson Rawls (F)
All Creatures Great and Small
  by James Herriot (NF)

If you like books about adventure...
Watership Down
  by Richard Adams (F)
Trapped
  by Marc Aronson (F)

If you like biographies...
I Am Malala
  by Malala Yousafzai (NF)
Women in Science: 50 Fearless Pioneers Who Changed the World
  by Rachel Ignotofsky (NF)

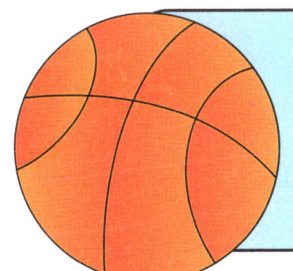

If you like sports...
Ghost
  by Jason Reynolds (F)
I Got This
  by Laurie Hernandez (NF)

If you like fantasy...
His Dark Materials: The Golden Compass
  by Philip Pullman (F)
Redwall
  by Brian Jacques (F)

If you like science...
Vanishing Life: The Mystery of Mass Extinctions
  by Jeff Hecht (NF)
Bugged: How Insects Changed History
  by Sarah Albee and Robert Leighton (NF)

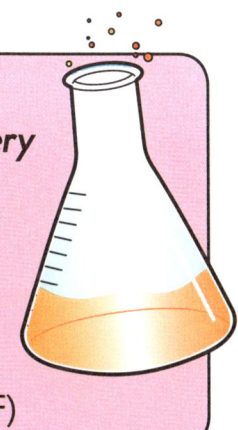

© Carson Dellosa Education

Summer Learning Is Everywhere!

Find learning opportunities wherever you go, all summer long!

Reading

- Find out if any of your favorite movies were based on or have book adaptations. Compare the books to the movies.
- Read three different news articles on the same topic from different sources.

Language Arts

- Work with a friend to make a magazine or newsletter about a shared interest.
- Practice writing in a journal. Experiment with different writing styles to find which you like more.

Math

- Plan a dream vacation and calculate how much it would cost. If your travel destination uses a different currency, be sure to convert the costs.
- Get information on how much gasoline costs near you and the average gas mileage for three different kinds of cars. Estimate how much a 100-mile road trip would cost for each car.

Science & Social Studies

- Choose a historical figure that you admire and research one way that they influenced the world today.
- Pick one natural phenomenon that you have observed during the summer. Come up with an explanation for the phenomenon and do research to find out if you were right.

Character & Fitness

- Write a list of the positive characteristics that your closest friend has and decide which traits you share.
- Find a more active way to accomplish something you do regularly. For example, try doing an exercise between chores.

© Carson Dellosa Education

SECTION 1

Monthly Goals

A goal is something that you want to accomplish and must work toward. Sometimes, reaching a goal can be difficult.

Think of three goals to set for yourself this month. For example, you may want to exercise for 30 minutes each day. Write your goals on the lines. Post them somewhere that you will see them every day.

Draw a check mark beside each goal you meet. Feel proud that you have met your goals and continue to set new ones to challenge yourself.

1. _____
2. _____
3. _____

Word List

The following words are used in this section. Use a dictionary to look up each word that you do not know. Then, write three sentences. Use at least one word from the word list in each sentence.

appreciated
auspicious
critical
foreboding
mingle

novel
ominous
perilous
secretion
trepidation

1. _____
2. _____
3. _____

SECTION I

Introduction to Flexibility

This section includes fitness and character development activities that focus on flexibility. These activities are designed to get you moving and thinking about building your physical fitness and your character.

Physical Flexibility

To the average person, *flexibility* means being able to accomplish everyday physical tasks easily, such as bending to tie a shoe. These everyday tasks can be difficult for people whose muscles and joints have not been used and stretched regularly.

Proper stretching allows muscles and joints to move through their full range of motion, which is important for good flexibility. There are many ways that you stretch every day without realizing it. When you reach for a dropped pencil or a box of cereal on the top shelf, you are stretching your muscles. Flexibility is important to your health, so challenge yourself to improve your flexibility consciously. Simple stretches and activities, such as yoga and tai chi, can improve your flexibility. Set a stretching goal for the summer, such as practicing daily until you can touch your toes.

Flexibility of Character

While it is important to have a flexible body, it is also important to be mentally flexible. Being mentally flexible means being open-minded about change. It can be disappointing when things do not go your way, but this is a normal reaction. Think of a time when unexpected circumstances ruined your recent plans. Maybe your mother had to work one weekend, and you could not go to a baseball game with friends because you needed to babysit a younger sibling. How did you deal with the situation?

A large part of being mentally flexible is realizing that there will be situations in life where unforeseen things happen. Often, it is how you react to the circumstances that affects the outcome. Arm yourself with tools to be flexible, such as having realistic expectations, brainstorming solutions to make a disappointing situation better, and looking for good things that may have resulted from the initial disappointment.

Mental flexibility can take many forms. For example, being fair, respecting the differences of other people, and being compassionate are ways that you can practice mental flexibility. In difficult situations, remind yourself to be flexible, and you will reap the benefits of this important character trait.

Measurement/Grammar

DAY 1

Find the surface area or volume of each rectangular prism. Show your work on a separate sheet of paper.

1.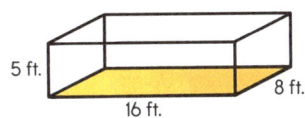

   SA = _____

2.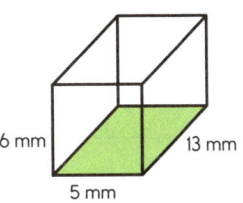

   SA = _____

3.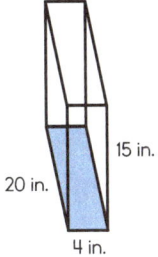

   SA = _____

4.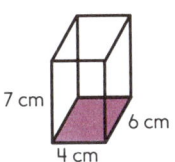

   V = _____

5.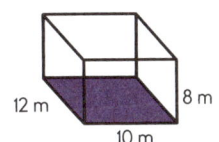

   V = _____

6.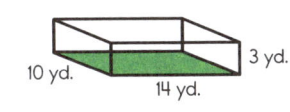

   V = _____

Read the passage. Underline each noun. Then, draw three lines under each letter that should be capitalized.

american pioneers followed several routes on their journeys west. Pioneers from new england traveled across new york on the mohawk trail. another route led through the cumberland gap, a natural pass in the appalachian mountains that ends near the borders of kentucky, tennessee, and virginia.

the first groups of settlers crossing the appalachian mountains in the late 1700s and early 1800s followed these early trails. The popular conestoga wagon, which originated in pennsylvania and was probably introduced by mennonite german settlers, carried many pioneers migrating southward through the Great appalachian valley along the Great wagon road.

DAY 1

Vocabulary/Science

Circle the letter next to the word that correctly completes each analogy.

7. desert : rain forest :: _____ : ravine
   A. ocean   B. canyon   C. plateau   D. mountain

8. tasteless : bland :: auspicious : _____
   A. foreboding   B. favorable   C. trepidation   D. suspicious

9. sight : eyes :: touch : _____
   A. play   B. fingers   C. feel   D. move

10. bird : nest :: rabbit : _____
    A. field   B. den   C. carrot   D. burrow

11. mobile phone : battery :: human : _____
    A. food   B. clothing   C. shelter   D. shoes

Write the letter of the word from the word bank that completes each sentence.

> A. cells   B. chlorophyll   C. chromosomes
> D. endoplasmic reticulum   E. organelles   F. nucleus
> G. interphase

12. _____ In the first stage of cell reproduction, the ____ disappears.
13. _____ Before mitosis begins, the cell's ____ , such as chloroplast and mitochondria, make copies of themselves.
14. _____ The period of time when a cell grows and copies its DNA is called ____.
15. _____ The basic units of structure in all living organisms are the ____.
16. _____ After mitosis, each identical daughter cell has a complete set of ____.
17. _____ Plant cells use ____ to capture sunlight.
18. _____ Materials and proteins are transported through the cells by the ____.

FACTOID: The first parking meter appeared in Oklahoma on July 16, 1935.

Geometry/Language Arts

DAY 2

Tell what shape is created by each cross section.

1.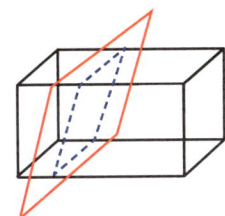
_____

2.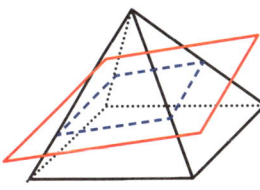
_____

3.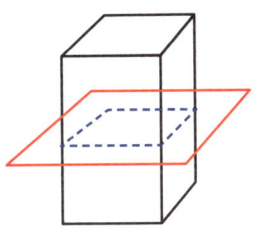
_____

4.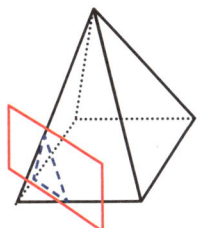
_____

Read each sentence. Add commas where they are needed between the different coordinate adjectives.

5. Lila has always felt competitive with her intelligent charming athletic older sister.
6. The heavy leather-bound antique dictionary had been passed down for four generations.
7. The nervous expectant mother was sure that her baby would arrive before morning.
8. The Goldsteins had driven hundreds of miles to see the majestic towering redwood trees.
9. Nazir picked nearly a bushel of juicy red apples.
10. It seemed only fitting that Monday began as a chilly gray drizzly day.
11. The clear blue water seemed to beckon to Rafael.
12. The brown spotted frog jumped onto a rock and sat there motionless all morning.
13. Juice from the plump ripe strawberries dribbled down Katrina's chin.
14. The eager excited fans cheered when the players jogged onto the field.

DAY 2

Vocabulary/Reading Comprehension

Read each word. Write *P* if the word has a positive connotation. Write *N* if the word has a negative connotation.

15. _____ annoy
16. _____ unique
17. _____ worthless
18. _____ clumsy
19. _____ compliment
20. _____ exquisite
21. _____ glorious
22. _____ cheerful

Read the passage. Then, answer the questions.

Primary and Secondary Sources

When you conduct research for a paper, you use many sources. A primary source may be a letter, a diary, an interview, a speech, or a law. A primary source provides firsthand information about an event from the view of someone who was present when that event occurred. A secondary source, such as an encyclopedia or a textbook, is a collection and interpretation of information gathered from other sources after an event has happened. If you look at the last page in an encyclopedia entry, you may see a list of articles and books that the author consulted. A letter written home from a soldier serving in World War II is a primary source. It might tell about his experiences with other soldiers in a foreign country. A book that examines the role of the United States during World War II is a secondary source. It might discuss several soldiers' letters and draw conclusions from them.

23. What is the main idea of this passage?
    A. A textbook is a secondary source.
    B. Primary sources are written by someone who was present at an event.
    C. Research includes the use of both primary and secondary sources.

24. What kind of information do primary sources provide? _____
    _____

25. What does a secondary source interpret? _____

26. Name a primary source you might use to write a research paper about the Klondike Gold Rush. _____

 **FITNESS FLASH:** Practice a V-sit. Stretch five times.

* See page ii.

Ratios/Vocabulary

DAY 3

Find the unit rate in each problem. Equivalent ratios are provided for the first problem. Solve for the variable.

1. A chef uses $4\frac{3}{4}$ cups of broth for 10 servings of soup. How much broth is used in one serving of soup? Let x represent the amount of broth.

    equivalent ratios: $\frac{4\frac{3}{4}}{10} = \frac{x}{1}$ _____ cups of broth per serving

2. Louisa biked $50\frac{4}{5}$ miles in 4 hours. How many miles did she bike per hour? Let m represent the number of miles.

    equivalent ratios: _____ _____ miles per hour

3. $124\frac{7}{8}$ gallons of water drained from a pool in 25 minutes. How much water drained from the pool each minute? Let g represent the number of gallons.

    equivalent ratios: _____ _____ gallons per minute

Look up each word in an online or print dictionary. Circle the syllable that is stressed. Then, write the word's part of speech and definition on the line. If it has more than one definition and part of speech, use the first one listed.

4. facilitate _____

5. mezzanine _____

6. accomplice _____

7. promulgate _____

8. patriarch _____

9. confiscate _____

10. utilitarian _____

DAY 3

Reading Comprehension

Read the passage. Then, answer the questions.

Dancing Honeybees

Many flowering plants depend on bees for pollination. When a honeybee discovers a patch of flowers with **nectar** and pollen, the bee flies to the hive to alert the other honeybees. The bee dances to communicate with the other bees in the hive.

The bee's dance is a code that explains the direction and distance of the flowers. The honeybee uses the sun as her point of reference. For example, if she performs her dance to the left of an imaginary vertical line perpendicular to the sun, this signals to the other bees that the location of the flowers is to the left of the sun. A long dance indicates a larger find, while a short dance signals a smaller discovery.

Within a short period of time, many worker bees leave the hive and head for the flowers. A honeybee can visit between 50 and 100 flowers during a single collection trip. The average honeybee produces about one-twelfth of a teaspoon of honey in her lifetime. Honeybees must visit about two million flowers to make one pound (0.45 kg) of honey.

11. Which of the following best defines the word *nectar*?
    A. flowers where bees stop and rest
    B. the sweet secretion from flowers
    C. the male bee
    D. the hive's location

12. Which of the following statements is false?
    A. A honeybee can visit 50 to 100 flowers during a single collection trip.
    B. Each worker bee produces about one pound (0.45 kg) of honey in a lifetime.
    C. The length of the dance signifies how large or small the find is.
    D. When a worker bee finds a patch of flowers, she shares the information with the other bees in the hive.

13. How does the second paragraph of the selection support the author's theme or main topic? _____
    _____
    _____

FACTOID: More than 7,000 languages are spoken in the world. Some are used by only a few people.

Algebra/Vocabulary

DAY 4

Use the equation $k = y \div x$ to find the constant of proportionality for the set of values below. Then, complete the table with three more values. Graph the points on the coordinate plane, draw a line through the points, and answer the question.

x	1	2	___	___	___
y	3	6	___	___	___

k =

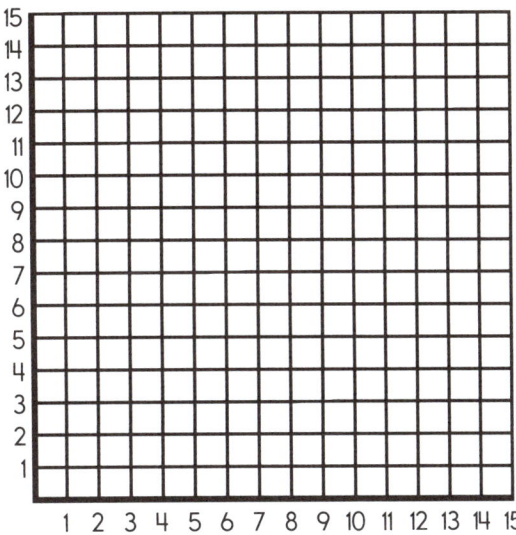

How does the graph show that the rate of change is constant? _____

Match each word with another word that has a similar denotation but a different connotation. Write the letter of the matching word on the line.

1. _____ skinny   a. aggressive
2. _____ fragrance   b. residence
3. _____ assertive   c. smirk
4. _____ smile   d. glower
5. _____ thrifty   e. clever
6. _____ home   f. odor
7. _____ stare   g. stingy
8. _____ shrewd   h. slender

DAY 4

Vocabulary/Writing

Use context clues to write the correct word from the word bank to complete each sentence.

| perilous | bulldozer | recipe | doze | breakfast | charcoal |

9. Of all the machines on the heavy-equipment lot, the _____ is the best to push sand and soil into a pile.

10. Because her neighbor's dog barked all night, Sarah was tired and started to _____ in her chair that morning.

11. It is _____ to chase a ball into the street when cars and other vehicles are approaching.

12. The _____ for brownies is in the striped cookbook.

13. Mrs. Frye's _____ consisted of boiled eggs and rye toast.

14. The artist used _____ to sketch the stream.

Create a new word. Write a definition for your new word. How do you pronounce it? How is it used? Write a sentence using your new word.

_____
_____
_____
_____
_____
_____
_____
_____

FITNESS FLASH: Touch your toes 10 times.

* See page ii.

Geometry/Probability

DAY 5

Find the length represented by x for each pair of similar triangles.

1.
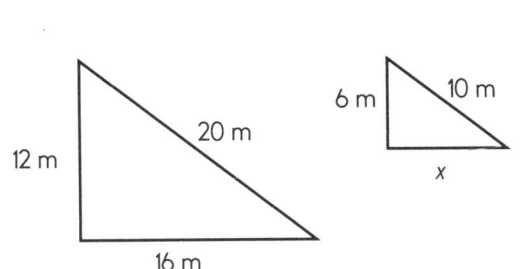

x = _____

2.
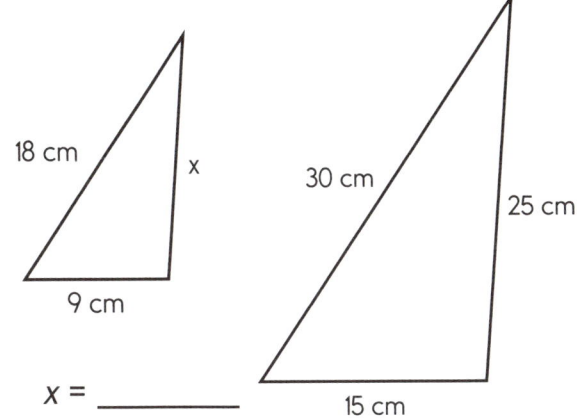

x = _____

3.
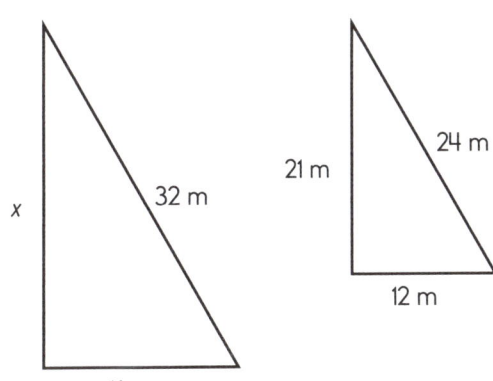

x = _____

4.
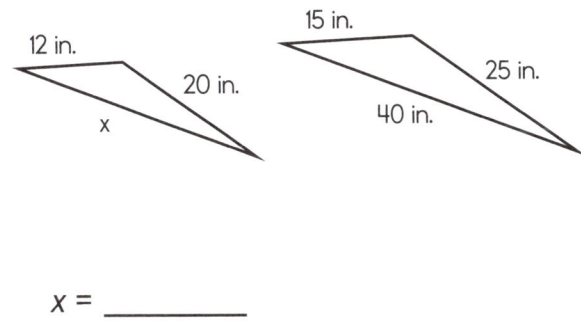

x = _____

Use the information below to determine the probability of each event occurring. Simplify if possible.

A die with sides numbered 1 to 6 is rolled. Find the probability of rolling each outcome.

5. P(5) = _____

6. P(1 or 2) = _____

7. P(odd number) = _____

8. P(not 6) = _____

9. P(even number) = _____

10. P(1, 2, 3, or 4) = _____

DAY 5

Vocabulary/Fitness

The way a word is used in a sentence can help you determine its meaning. Read each sentence. Circle the correct meaning of each boldfaced word as it is used in the sentence.

11. That antique painting has **appreciated** over time.
    A. increased in value
    B. felt grateful for

12. A good education is **critical** for success later in life.
    A. disapproving
    B. important

13. The banker deposited $500 in the **vault**.
    A. a piece of gymnastic equipment
    B. a large safe

14. We enjoyed the **sparkling** conversation at the party.
    A. glittering
    B. interesting

15. Reyna put the horse in the **stall** after she groomed him.
    A. area of the barn
    B. halt or pause

16. Matthew thought of a **novel** approach to solving his problem.
    A. new or innovative
    B. fictional book

Hoop Twist

Have you ever watched someone swing a golf club or a baseball bat? Professional golfers and baseball players regularly work on their flexibility so that they have a broader range of motion. This allows them to hit the ball farther. Use a large hoop (or an exercise band or towel) to increase your back's range of motion. Step inside the hoop. Lift it to waist height. Hold the hoop against your back, hands spread wide apart. Gently move the hoop around your body with your hands. Your arms will twist at the shoulders from the sides of your body to the front and back. Now, move the hoop in the other direction. Keep your feet firmly planted on the floor and hips facing forward. Only your torso should move. Start slowly until you feel your muscles loosening. If using an exercise band or a towel, keep your arms in front of you and twist your torso.

CHARACTER CHECK: Think of a game you like to play. Write a TV or radio commercial promoting fairness while playing the game.

* See page ii.

Data Analysis/Grammar

DAY 6

Amanda asked each student in her class: *How many pets do you have?* The data she collected is below.

Amanda's Class:	0, 0, 2, 1, 1, 0, 5, 0, 3, 2, 1, 1, 0, 2, 4, 0, 2, 1, 1, 1, 2, 3, 1, 0, 2

Charley asked the same question to each student in his class (which is not the same class as Amanda's). The data he collected is below.

Charley's Class:	1, 2, 1, 3, 1, 1, 0, 0, 1, 0, 0, 2, 3, 1, 2, 5, 2, 0, 0, 4, 1, 1, 2, 0, 0, 1, 1, 2, 0

Answer the questions based on Amanda's and Charley's data.

1. Whose class had a larger percentage of students with no pets? _____
2. Who surveyed a larger population? _____
3. Based on Amanda's data, about how many students per class will have 3 or more pets? _____
4. If a third class of 30 students were surveyed, predict about how many students would have 1 pet. _____

A *predicate nominative* is a noun or pronoun that follows a linking verb and renames or describes the sentence's subject. Read each sentence. Underline the predicate nominative once. Underline the linking verb twice. Then, draw an arrow from the predicate nominative to the subject it renames.

5. *The Book Thief* by Markus Zusak is a novel for teens that is set in Germany during World War II.
6. Charles Dickens is the author of the novel *Great Expectations*.
7. One of the main characters in J. R. R. Tolkien's book *The Fellowship of the Ring* is a wizard named Gandalf.
8. Homer's story *The Iliad* is a classic tale about the Trojan War.
9. *Harry Potter and the Sorcerer's Stone* is the first book in a series by J. K. Rowling.
10. *The Westing Game* by Ellen Raskin is a popular book.
11. *Animal Farm* and *1984* are two famous novels by George Orwell.

DAY 6

Reading Comprehension

Read the passage. Then, answer the questions.

The Great Compromise

When the Founding Fathers wrote the U. S. Constitution, they debated about how many representatives each state should have in the federal government. They proposed a plan that states with larger populations should have more votes in Congress than smaller states. This was called the Virginia Plan. However, states with smaller populations disagreed with this plan. They wanted each state to have an equal number of representatives so that less-populated states would have as much say as the more populated states. Their plan was called the New Jersey Plan. After further debate, lawmakers suggested a compromise called the Connecticut Plan. The Connecticut Plan called for a bicameral legislature, or a two-house Congress. One house, called the Senate, would have the same number of representatives from each state. The other house, called the House of Representatives, would have a different number of representatives from each state, based on the state's population. The Connecticut Plan pleased both large and small states and became known as the Great Compromise.

12. Why did the less-populated states disagree with the Virginia Plan? _____
_____
_____
_____

13. Why did the more-populated states think the Virginia Plan was fair? _____
_____

14. What is a compromise? _____

15. Do you think it is important for people in the government to compromise? Why or why not? _____
_____

16. Write about a time when you had to compromise with someone. _____
_____

FACTOID: About 70 percent of Earth's species are found in just 12 countries: Australia, Brazil, China, Colombia, Ecuador, India, Indonesia, Madagascar, Mexico, Peru, and Zaire.

Geometry/Grammar

DAY 7

Use the figure to the right to list all of the pairs of angles that fit each description.

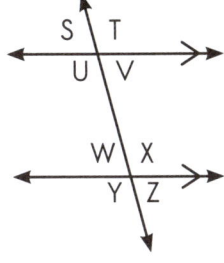

1. alternate exterior angles _____
2. alternate interior angles _____
3. consecutive interior angles _____
4. corresponding angles _____
5. vertical angles _____
6. adjacent angles (name two pairs) _____

Use the figure to the right to identify each pair of angles as alternate exterior, alternate interior, consecutive interior, or corresponding.

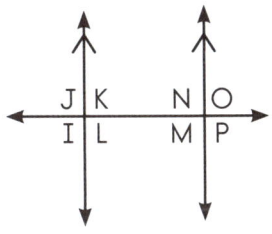

7. ∠I and ∠M are _____ angles.
8. ∠J and ∠P are _____ angles.
9. ∠K and ∠M are _____ angles.
10. ∠L and ∠M are _____ angles.
11. ∠I and ∠O are _____ angles.
12. ∠K and ∠O are _____ angles.

A *direct object* is a noun or a pronoun in the predicate that receives the action of the verb. A direct object answers the question *whom* or *what*. Circle the direct object in each sentence.

13. Every person needs an outlet for frustration.
14. Who sent me the mystery gift?
15. My mom bought a new bracelet on the Internet.
16. Joseph has recorded the minutes of the board meetings for the past 20 years.
17. Samuel Clemens portrayed life on the Mississippi River during the 1800s through the eyes of his characters, Tom Sawyer and Huckleberry Finn.
18. Should we send Kia roses for winning the district high jump competition?
19. Every student in the class enjoys Miss Osbourne because of her wonderful sense of humor and upbeat presentations.
20. After graduating from college, Cindy plans a career in medicine.

DAY 7

Vocabulary/Critical Thinking

Circle the letter of the correct meaning for each root word.

21. cred
    A. above
    B. believe
    C. feel

22. photo
    A. light
    B. free
    C. shape

23. morph
    A. love
    B. form
    C. change

24. alter
    A. make
    B. send
    C. other

25. port
    A. carry
    B. out
    C. in

26. script
    A. give
    B. write
    C. touch

Nick, Joey, Beki, and Carmen ran in the town's annual road race. Each person had a different jersey number (2, 13, 20, and 34) and finished in a different amount of time (10 minutes, 11 minutes, 12 minutes, and 14 minutes). Use the information and deductive reasoning to determine each person's jersey number and race time.

- The runner with the lowest jersey number also ran the slowest time.
- Nick's jersey number is 18 greater than Carmen's.
- Of the four runners, a man had the fastest finishing time.
- The sum of the digits on Beki's jersey number is 7.
- Nick finished exactly 2 minutes faster than Beki.

	2	13	20	34
Nick				
Joey				
Beki				
Carmen				

FITNESS FLASH: Do arm circles for 30 seconds.

* See page ii.

Probability/Grammar

DAY 8

Use the given probability to predict long-term outcomes. Round the answers to whole numbers.

1. The probability of pulling a red marble out of bag of colored marbles is 3:7. If you were to pull colored marbles out of the bag (one at a time, and putting the marble back each time) for 500 tries, approximately how many times would you select a red marble?

    _____ times

2. The probability of spinning a 7 on a spinner is 0.083. If you spun 250 times, approximately how many times would the spinner land on 7?

    _____ times

3. The probability of drawing an ace from a deck of cards is $\frac{1}{13}$. If you drew one card at a time (and put the card back each time) for 400 tries, how many times total could you expect to draw an ace?

    _____ times

An *indirect object* precedes the direct object and tells *to whom* or *for whom* the action of the verb is done. It also answers the question *who*. Circle the indirect object in each sentence.

4. Mr. Hanson taught the class a lesson in democracy.
5. The parts company will ship them the package by Friday.
6. If I give you the money, will you buy a T-shirt at the concert for me?
7. My dad began paying me an allowance when I was in eighth grade.
8. The Smith family prepared us a delicious meal.
9. Every student in Coach Steinman's P.E. class gave him a card or a small gift when he retired.
10. Marie Curie's radiation research earned her a Nobel Prize in 1903.
11. Our art class bought Miss Sherman a bouquet of flowers for being such a wonderful and caring teacher.
12. Bonnie showed the volunteers the donations for the canned food drive.
13. I built my brother a go-cart for the annual race.

DAY 8

Literary Terms

An *idiom* is a phrase that has a different meaning than the literal meaning of each word within the expression. Underline the idiom in each sentence. Then, write what you think the idiom means.

14. When it came to political differences, Mr. Jackson drew a line in the sand.
    _____

15. Keep your shirt on! We are almost there.
    _____

16. The motor on our boat went belly up.
    _____

17. I don't see how you can keep a straight face.
    _____

18. The 100-meter dash ended in a dead heat.
    _____

19. Andrew walked through the glassware store like a bull in a china shop.
    _____

20. After spending 10 days on a beach in Hawaii, Paula returned to work and began to wade through the stack of papers on her desk.
    _____

21. During the holiday party, employees jockeyed for position to shake hands with the company president.
    _____

FACTOID: Baseball's first World Series was played in 1903 between the Boston Red Sox and the Pittsburgh Pirates.

Probability/Grammar

DAY 9

Complete the table to determine the total number of possible outcomes.

At a sandwich shop, customers can choose one item from each column for the total price of $3.99. How many sandwich combinations are available at that price?

Choose a bread.	Choose a filling.	Choose a cheese.
white rye pumpernickel	ham turkey tofu	Swiss cheddar provolone

white			rye			pumpernickel		
ham	turkey	tofu						

There are _____ possible outcomes.

Combine each pair of sentences with a conjunction.

1. I arrived late for the interview. My alarm clock didn't go off on time. _____

2. My cousin Jen arrived at six o'clock. We immediately began setting up the board game. _____

3. The restaurant on Colony Road was closed. We ate at the diner across the road instead. _____

4. We have no need to ration the fruit. We have several containers of raspberries and cherries. _____

DAY 9

Reading Comprehension

Read the poem. Then, answer the questions.

Much of Robert Frost's work, like this **pastoral** poem, describes the life and landscapes of rural New England, where he spent much of his life.

Going for Water by Robert Frost

The well was dry beside the door,
And so we went with pail and can
Across the fields behind the house
To seek the brook if still it ran;

Not loth to have excuse to go,   5
Because the autumn eve was fair
(Though chill), because the fields were ours,
And by the brook our woods were there.

We ran as if to meet the moon   9
That slowly dawned behind the trees,
The barren boughs without the leaves,
Without the birds, without the breeze.

But once within the wood, we paused   13
Like gnomes that hid us from the moon,
Ready to run to hiding new
With laughter when she found us soon.

Each laid on other a staying hand   17
To listen ere we dared to look,
And in the hush we joined to make
We heard, we knew we heard the brook.

A note as from a single place,   21
A slender tinkling fall that made
Now drops that floated on the pool
Like pearls, and now a silver blade.

5. What does *pastoral* mean? Which words in the poem support this description?

_____

6. Based on the poem's tone, how do the characters feel about fetching the water?

_____

7. In line 16, who does *she* refer to? _____

8. Frost structures this poem in *quatrains*, or stanzas of four lines each. What effect does this form have on the poem and how you read it? _____

_____

Probability/Grammar

DAY 10

Use the following information to determine the probability (P) of each event occurring. Simplify if possible.

A jar contains 18 jelly beans: 7 purple jelly beans, 3 green jelly beans, and 8 orange jelly beans. Without looking, Travis picks 1 jelly bean from the jar. What is the probability of each of the following outcomes?

1. P(green) = _____
2. P(purple) = _____
3. P(orange) = _____
4. P(not green) = _____
5. P(purple or green) = _____
6. P(not orange) = _____

An *appositive* is a noun, a pronoun, or a noun phrase that usually follows another noun or pronoun and describes it. The phrase is set off by commas. Combine each pair of sentences so that the new sentence has an appositive.

7. Anna got the lead role in the play. Anna is a great actress. _____
   _____
   _____

8. The United Nations is based in New York City. The United Nations is an influential international organization. _____
   _____
   _____

9. Bridget and Connor work at the Field Museum in Chicago, Illinois. Bridget and Connor are both geologists. _____
   _____
   _____

DAY 10

Vocabulary/Character Development

Use a print or online thesaurus to find and write a synonym for each word below.

10. cumbersome _____
11. depleted _____
12. derisive _____
13. prosperity _____
14. inane _____
15. equilibrium _____
16. subvert _____
17. commemorate _____
18. hirsute _____
19. trite _____

Showing Compassion

Compassion is the act of understanding and being kind to other living beings. There are many ways to show compassion. Treating animals humanely, being empathetic to the misfortune of others, forgiving others, and showing kindness and respect to everyone are just a few ways to show compassion.

Brainstorm a list of ways that you can demonstrate compassion in your community. Consider organizations that need volunteers, make a list of items you no longer need that can be donated, or think of your own project to benefit others living in or near your community. Discuss your list with a parent or family member. Then, put one of your ideas into action this summer.

CHARACTER CHECK: Watch for people who are demonstrating kindness. At the end of the day, share your observations with a family member.

Measurement/Parts of Speech

DAY 11

Find the circumference of each circle. Use 3.14 for π.

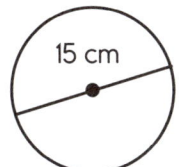 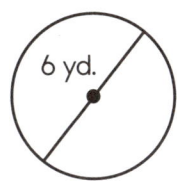 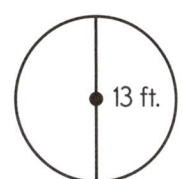 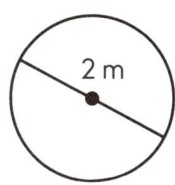

1. _____   2. _____   3. _____   4. _____

Find the area of each circle. Use 3.14 for π.

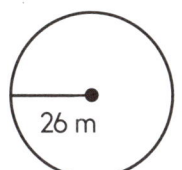 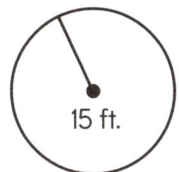  

5. _____   6. _____   7. _____   8. _____

A personal pronoun takes the place of a person or thing. An indefinite pronoun refers generally to a person or a thing. A demonstrative pronoun refers to a specific person or thing. Underline the pronoun in each sentence and identify it. Write *P* for personal, *I* for indefinite, or *D* for demonstrative.

9. _____ Chelsea knows everyone in the room.
10. _____ You are a good photographer.
11. _____ He is running in the race on Saturday.
12. _____ Daniel's father helped them find the keys.
13. _____ It broke yesterday.
14. _____ Lincoln will play tennis with you.
15. _____ Neither was prepared for the pop quiz.
16. _____ They filled the stadium to listen to the candidate speak.
17. _____ These are the items for the canned food drive.
18. _____ I won't go unless Kate goes.
19. _____ That is the easiest way to solve the problem.
20. _____ Many liked the pizza with homemade crust and extra cheese.
21. _____ This is the jacket that Tasha wants.
22. _____ Does anybody know what time it is?

DAY 11

Language Arts/Social Studies

Read each description and write the corresponding source from the word bank.

| newspaper or magazine | atlas | encyclopedia |
| almanac | nonfiction books | Internet |

23. contains Web sites about nearly any subject _____
24. contains maps, facts, and figures about various geographical features and locations _____
25. contains historical and/or statistical information _____
26. contains up-to-date information about current topics, often organized by issue _____
27. organizes facts and information, often alphabetically _____
28. autobiographies, biographies, and other factual information _____

Write the letter of the word from the word bank that matches each description.

| A. canyon | B. dune | C. isthmus | D. plateau | E. savanna |
| F. delta | G. tributary | H. oasis | I. reef | J. strait |

29. _____ a sandy hill formed by the wind
30. _____ triangular-shaped land formed by silt deposits at the mouth of a river
31. _____ a fertile area in a desert with a steady water supply
32. _____ a narrow body of water that connects two larger bodies of water
33. _____ a narrow, deep valley with steep sides
34. _____ a large, high, flat area that rises above the surrounding land
35. _____ flat, open grassland with scattered trees and shrubs
36. _____ a smaller river or stream that flows into a larger one
37. _____ a narrow strip of land connecting two larger landmasses
38. _____ sand, rock, or coral at or near the surface of the water

FACTOID: The Nile River is 4,132 miles (6,650 km) long.

Problem Solving/Parts of Speech

DAY 12

Solve each problem.

1. The regular price of a pair of pants is $38.00. The pants are discounted 35%. How much do the pants cost after the discount is applied? _____

2. A bookstore is having a sale. The book Bart wants was originally priced at $14.99. The book is now $10.04. By what percentage was the price reduced? _____

3. Lisa dined at a restaurant and gave the waiter a 15% tip. If the price of her meal was $10.25, how much did Lisa tip the waiter? _____

4. Emily bought a new car for $22,000. She paid 93% of the list price. How much was the list price? _____

A *relative pronoun* connects a group of words to a noun or a pronoun. An interrogative pronoun introduces a question. Read each sentence. Write *R* if the underlined pronoun is relative. Write *I* if the underlined pronoun is interrogative.

5. _____ I will bring whatever you need.
6. _____ What time is your appointment?
7. _____ Which poster won the contest?
8. _____ The essay, which was written by Alyssa, won first place.
9. _____ Choose whichever restaurant you want.
10. _____ What is the title of that song?
11. _____ I don't know what she said.
12. _____ Who brought the chips and juice to the party?
13. _____ I will always remember the nurse who helped me.
14. _____ The child, whom I saw at the parade, was eight years old.

FITNESS FLASH: Do 10 shoulder shrugs.

* See page ii.

DAY 12

Literary Terms/Writing

Point of view is the perspective from which a story is told. If a writer tells a story from the first-person point of view, the writer uses *I*. If a writer tells a story from the third-person point of view, the writer uses *he, she*, or *they*. Read each sentence. Decide from whose point of view the sentence is being told. Write *F* for first person or *T* for third person.

15. _____ I played a tune on my new harmonica.
16. _____ When the clock struck eight, they walked into town to hear the concert in the square.
17. _____ Sulking, she used her umbrella to shield herself from the rain.
18. _____ I imagined myself as a great singer, performing on stage for a large audience.
19. _____ On a whim, he planted the red geranium in the clay flowerpot.
20. _____ Reading the inscription on the plaque, I was amazed by the building's fascinating history.
21. _____ I speculated that my sister was allergic to the new laundry detergent because of the rash on her arms.

Describe what a typical day would be like from your hand's point of view. How would the world seem different from your hand's perspective?

_____
_____
_____
_____
_____
_____
_____
_____

 **FITNESS FLASH:** Practice a V-sit. Stretch five times.

* See page ii.

Algebra/Geometry

DAY 13

Use the order of operations to solve each problem.

1. 2 × 3[7 + (6 ÷ 2)] = _____
2. 3[-3(2 – 8) – 6] = _____
3. 3 × 3[2 – (9 ÷ 3)] = _____
4. 2[-5(4 – 12) – 3] = _____
5. [(3 × 3) – (30 ÷ 6)] + (-27) – 13 = _____
6. 2 ÷ [(4 ÷ 2) + (32 ÷ 8)] = _____

Label each type of triangle using a word from the word bank.

| right | obtuse | acute | scalene | isosceles |

7. side lengths are 3 cm, 4 cm, and 6 cm _____
8. angles measure 40°, 60°, and 80° _____
9. angles measure 25°, 10°, and 145° _____
10. side lengths are 6 in., 5 in., and 6 in. _____
11. angles measure 30°, 60°, and 90° _____

Use a protractor to draw each triangle according to the description.

12. A right triangle with one angle that is 50°

13. An isosceles triangle with a 35° angle and a 110° angle

DAY 13

Read the playbill. Then, answer the questions.

> *Belle of the Ball: A Comedy in Two Acts*
> by Elizabeth Weaver
>
> **Cast:** (in order of appearance)
> Elizabeth Brown..Lucy Scott
> Belle Brown..Meg Mitchell
> Dressmaker..Susan Moore
> Mr. Brown..Grant Jordan
> Mrs. Brown..Jennifer Mills
> Ernest Enderby...Michael Thompson
> Clover, the family cat...Clover
> Partygoers: Ben Adams, Ann Davis, Chandra King, Andy Miller, Susan Moore
>
> ## ACT I
>
> **Time:** mid-afternoon
> **Setting:** 1920s, the Brown family home
>
> Elizabeth and Belle are in their bedroom preparing for their family's annual ball. The dressmaker is adjusting Elizabeth's gown. Belle is putting the finishing touches on her dress. Mr. and Mrs. Brown talk with Ernest Enderby. Clover emerges from her hiding place under the sofa.
>
> ## ACT II
>
> **Time:** evening
> **Setting:** the ballroom
>
> Elizabeth and Belle **mingle** with the partygoers. Belle leads the dancing until the ball is unexpectedly disrupted. The guests gather outside. Ernest Enderby makes an announcement.

14. Which actor plays more than one role?
    A. Grant Jordan
    B. Lucy Scott
    C. Susan Moore

15. Which of the following best defines the word *mingle*?
    A. dance
    B. take pictures of
    C. socialize

16. What is the setting for Act II? _____

FACTOID: The average temperature on Mars is -81°F (-63°C).

Algebra/Parts of Speech

DAY 14

Solve each problem.

1. −233 − (−233) = _____
2. 31 − (−8) = _____
3. −103 − (−575) = _____
4. −16 − (−38) = _____
5. 43 + (−56) − 78 = _____
6. −78 − 65 = _____
7. −19 − 4 = _____
8. −16 + 9 = _____
9. 71 + (−18) = _____
10. 0 − 17 = _____
11. −8 + (−5) = _____
12. 12 + (−7) = _____
13. −13 + 26 = _____
14. −9 − (−24) = _____
15. 0 − (−9) = _____

A pronoun in the nominative case is a subject, a predicate nominative, or an appositive. A pronoun in the objective case is the object of a verb or a preposition. Circle the pronoun in parentheses that correctly completes each sentence. Then, identify its case. Write *N* for nominative or *O* for objective.

16. _____ One February afternoon, (we, us) went sledding.
17. _____ (She, Her) needs to finish her homework.
18. _____ Most of the students voted for (he, him) to be class president.
19. _____ (They, Them) are our best volleyball players.
20. _____ Call (I, me) when you get home.
21. _____ Please take the gift to (she, her).
22. _____ (They, Them) looked at the map.
23. _____ The teacher helped (he, him) with the math problem.
24. _____ The usher escorted (they, them) to their seats.
25. _____ She sat next to Amy and (I, me).

DAY 14

Reading Comprehension/Writing

When you describe the similarities between people, things, or events, you compare them. When you describe their differences, you contrast them. Read the passage and think about the comparisons and contrasts. Then, answer the questions.

Amphibians and reptiles are both cold-blooded animals. Both live in many different areas of the world. Reptiles lay hard-shelled eggs, but amphibians lay soft, sticky eggs. When reptiles hatch, they look like tiny adults. However, amphibians change their appearance throughout several life stages before they finally achieve their mature, adult forms.

26. What two things are being compared in this passage? _____
_____

27. How are the two things similar? How are they different? _____
_____
_____
_____

Would you rather have X-ray vision or the ability to fly? What would you do with each ability? What are their advantages and disadvantages? Explain how you made your choice. Use another piece of paper if you need more space.

_____
_____
_____
_____
_____
_____
_____
_____

FITNESS FLASH: Touch your toes 10 times.

* See page ii.

Algebra/Parts of Speech

DAY 15

Solve each problem.

1. (625 ÷ 5) × 0.2 = _____

2. 83 + (-85) = _____

3. $\frac{150}{-5}$ × (-4) = _____

4. (-34) + (-255) = _____

5. 80 – (-22) = _____

6. 28 – (-65) = _____

7. $\frac{-555}{-5}$ × (-6) = _____

8. 28 – (-26) = _____

9. -3 × 5 = _____

10. [-19 – (-20) – (-34)] ÷ (-6) = _____

11. $\frac{-424}{4}$ = _____

12. [-18 – (-66) – 22] × 2 = _____

13. 19 – 23 = _____

14. -61 – (-21) = _____

15. ($\frac{-72}{9}$) + ($\frac{-64}{8}$) + ($\frac{44}{-11}$) = _____

16. (16 – 21 + 34) ÷ (-8) = _____

Read the paragraph. Replace each underlined noun by writing a pronoun above it. Then, read the new paragraph.

Stepping off the plane, Mrs. Jackson arrived in Costa Rica at noon. As soon as <u>Mrs. Jackson</u> got to her hotel, <u>Mrs. Jackson</u> enjoyed a light lunch at the restaurant. After lunch, Mr. Jackson, who had taken a different flight, joined <u>Mrs. Jackson</u>. "Let's go to the beach," <u>Mr. Jackson</u> said. <u>Mr. and Mrs. Jackson</u> changed into swimsuits, and off <u>Mr. and Mrs. Jackson</u> went. That evening, <u>Mr. and Mrs. Jackson</u> called <u>Mr. and Mrs. Jackson's</u> son, Max. "<u>Mr. and Mrs. Jackson</u> are having a great time," <u>Mr. and Mrs. Jackson</u> told <u>Max</u>.

DAY 15

Literary Terms/Fitness

Write the correct word from the word bank to complete each sentence.

> drama   fable   fantasy   folklore   horror   legend

17. A _____ is usually written for theatrical performance.
18. A _____ demonstrates a useful truth and often includes talking animals.
19. A _____ invites readers to suspend reality.
20. _____ is usually passed from generation to generation by word of mouth and includes the stories of a people or culture.
21. _____ stories evoke an ominous feeling or dread in both the characters and the reader.
22. A _____ often features a national hero and may be based on real events.

Tree of Balance

Balance and flexibility are important in many sports, from tennis and skiing to football and horseback riding. Try this yoga tree pose, and you will be on your way to having greater balance and flexibility, as well as strength and endurance!

Stand straight with your feet hip-width apart. Raise your arms to the sides at shoulder height. Shift all of your weight to your left leg. Lift your right foot and rotate your knee to the side. Then, touch your right foot to your lower left leg or inner thigh without resting it on your knee. Now, raise your arms straight above your head. Hold this pose for 10 seconds. Slowly bring down your arms and foot. Try the other leg. Think of the foot on the ground as the roots of a tree; press it firmly into the ground. Your arms are the branches. Reach them toward the sky. For better balance, focus your eyes on a fixed point in front of you.

> **CHARACTER CHECK:** Why is honesty important? Write a 30-second commercial promoting honesty. Share it with a family member.

* See page ii.

Problem Solving/Vocabulary

DAY 16

Calculate unit rates to solve each problem. Round answers as needed.

1. Sabra went for a long hike and burned 845 calories in $3\frac{1}{4}$ hours. Nelson decided to go for a bike ride. He burned 1,435 calories in $4\frac{7}{8}$ hours. Who burned the most calories per hour?

   Unit rate for Sabra: _____   Unite rate for Nelson: _____

   _____ burned more calories per hour.

2. Stephan can run 3 miles in 15.75 minutes. Kelsha can run 5 miles in 22.6 minutes. Who can run faster?

   Unit rate for Stephan: _____   Unite rate for Kelsha: _____

   _____ runs faster.

3. Natalie went to Store A and bought $3\frac{4}{5}$ pounds of pistachios for $17.75. Nicholas went to Store B and bought $4\frac{7}{10}$ pounds of pistachios for $19.50. Who got the better deal?

   Unit rate for Natalie: _____   Unite rate for Nicholas: _____

   _____ got the better deal.

Use the context of each sentence to help you determine the meaning of the underlined word. Write the meaning on the line. Then, look up the word in a print or online dictionary to double-check the definition.

4. We were hoping that the rain would <u>abate</u> before Nicki's soccer game.

   _____

5. Mr. Gregor <u>reprimanded</u> the entire class for our behavior on the field trip.

   _____

6. The interviewer was impressed with Jamilla's <u>poise</u> and confidence.

   _____

7. William was <u>distraught</u> when he heard the news of his grandmother's illness.

   _____

8. The <u>acrid</u> smell of the smoke filled Alexi's lungs as he ran for the door.

   _____

DAY 16

Read the passage. Then, answer the questions.

Types of Rocks

Rocks are classified as igneous, sedimentary, or metamorphic, depending on how they were formed. Igneous rocks form when volcanoes erupt and release a molten rock material called *magma*. After the magma cools, it forms solid igneous rock. One type of igneous rock is granite, a very hard material often used in construction. Sedimentary rocks form when water deposits sediment, or small pieces of rocks and sand. Over time, sediment compresses into layers. These layers form sedimentary rock, such as limestone. Sedimentary rock often contains fossils and shells. Metamorphic rocks are the least common rock variety. Metamorphic rocks, such as marble, begin as igneous or sedimentary rocks that are squeezed tightly within Earth's crust over a long time.

9. What is the main idea of this passage?
    A. Hard rocks can be useful for building sturdy structures.
    B. There are three types of rock that are formed in different ways.
    C. Not all rocks look the same.

10. What are the three types of rocks? _____

11. How do igneous rocks form? _____

12. How do sedimentary rocks form? _____

13. How do metamorphic rocks form? _____

FACTOID: The muscles that move the eyes contract an average of 100,000 times each day.

Decimals & Fractions/Grammar

DAY 17

Rewrite each rational number as a decimal number. Round as needed. Mark digits that repeat by drawing a line over them.

EXAMPLE: $\frac{25}{99} = .\overline{25}$

1. $\frac{125}{100} =$ _____
2. $\frac{5}{12} =$ _____
3. $\frac{7}{10} =$ _____
4. $\frac{2}{3} =$ _____
5. $\frac{3}{9} =$ _____
6. $\frac{7}{8} =$ _____

An *independent clause* expresses a complete thought. A *dependent clause* has a subject and a verb but does not express a complete thought. Read each clause. Write *I* if it is an independent clause. Write *D* if it is a dependent clause.

7. _____ When Buster grew tired of chasing after the ball
8. _____ She was not fearful of the dentist during her checkup this year
9. _____ I have a great deal of respect for people with character
10. _____ Because she cannot help crying at sad movies

Circle each independent clause and underline each dependent clause.

11. I want to be the first to volunteer whenever the teacher asks for help.
12. If you stay until the birthday party is over, call Mom for a ride home.
13. When monsoon season begins, the humidity makes the air uncomfortable.
14. Pizza is Crawford's choice for dinner, but only if it has a thin crust.

A *complex sentence* contains one independent clause and one or more dependent clauses. Underline each independent clause and circle each dependent clause.

15. We stopped playing and sought shelter when the storm began.
16. Gabe hopped off his skateboard so that his friend could use it.
17. We won the state championship because we played together as a team.
18. Although the price of gasoline rose by 50 cents per gallon, Americans did not curb their travel plans.
19. If we fail to finish our project tonight, we will not be in Mrs. Hooper's good graces tomorrow.

DAY 17

Literary Terms/Social Studies

Write a word from the word bank to complete each sentence.

mystery	poetry	essay	biography	myth

20. A _____ often involves the solution of a crime.
21. A _____ often attempts to explain some natural phenomena and involves the actions of the gods.
22. Verse or rhythmic writing that creates an emotional response is called _____ .
23. A _____ is a factual account of a real person's life.
24. An _____ is a short composition that reflects the author's point of view.

Write the word from the word bank that matches each description.

capital resources	supply	scarcity
demand	inflation	services
goods	natural resources	

25. materials produced for sale _____
26. jobs that people perform for payment _____
27. the amount of goods or services purchased at a given price _____
28. things in nature that have a commercial use or value _____
29. an increase in the average cost of goods and services _____
30. machinery or equipment that produces other goods _____
31. the amount of a product available for sale _____
32. not enough goods and services available to meet demand _____

FITNESS FLASH: Do arm circles for 30 seconds.

* See page ii.

Algebra/Grammar

DAY 18

Add the expressions.

1. $(2x + 5) + (x + 4) =$ _____
2. $(3y - 5) + (2y + 4) =$ _____
3. $(4a + 12) + (-6a - 13) =$ _____

Subtract the expressions.

4. $(3x + 3) - (4x + 6) =$ _____
5. $(8y - 7) - (y - 4) =$ _____
6. $(3b + 6) - (-2b + 7) =$ _____

Factor each expression.

7. $16y - 8$ _____
8. $18x^2 - 9x$ _____
9. $-12c - 8$ _____

A simple sentence, or independent clause, contains a subject and a predicate and expresses a complete thought. A compound sentence contains two simple sentences joined by a conjunction. Read each sentence. Write *S* if the sentence is simple. Write *C* if the sentence is compound.

10. _____ Alyson and her sister Samantha have completely different interests.
11. _____ The telephone rang, and the doorbell buzzed at the same time.
12. _____ Both the canoe and the sailboat belong to Uncle Bill and Aunt Nancy.
13. _____ You bring the sandwiches, and I'll bring the chips and fruit.
14. _____ Lesley Mitchell finished her project ahead of schedule, but she didn't submit it to her English teacher until the due date.
15. _____ You should get your bike and join our trip.
16. _____ Many of the early settlers had never been farmers, and they were not prepared for the harsh New England winters.
17. _____ Camilla stayed longer than usual.
18. _____ Really great movies are hard to find, but I'm not very picky.
19. _____ Luke goes home and studies every day after school.

DAY 18

Geometry/Science

Use the figure to the right to answer each question.

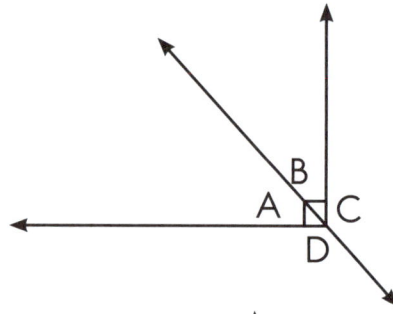

20. m∠A + m∠B = _____°

    ∠A and ∠B are _____ angles.

21. m∠D + m∠ _____ = 180°

    ∠D and ∠A are _____ angles.

Use the figure to the right to answer each question.

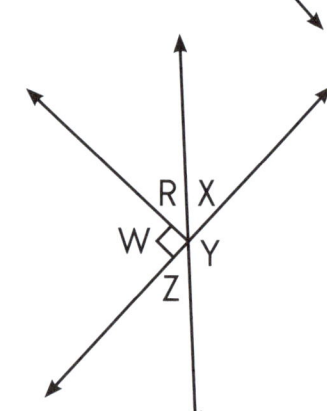

22. If m∠X = 45°, m∠R = _____°, m∠Y = _____°,

    and m∠Z = _____°

23. m∠X + m∠Y = _____°

24. m∠R + m∠X = _____°

25. ∠R and ∠X are _____ angles.

Use the words in the word bank to label the paramecium, an animal-like protist.

| anal pore | oral groove | food vacuole | cytoplasm |
| micronucleus | cilia | macronucleus | cell membrane |

26. _____
27. _____
28. _____
29. _____
30. _____
31. _____
32. _____
33. _____

FACTOID: One-third of the people on Earth live in China and India.

Multiplication & Division/Parts of Speech

DAY 19

Find each product or quotient. Round answers as needed.

1. 12.5 × 5.8 = _____
2. $\frac{4}{9} \div \left(-\frac{3}{10}\right)$ = _____
3. $-3\frac{1}{7} \div 10\frac{4}{5}$ = _____
4. $-3\frac{1}{5} \times \left(-7\frac{3}{8}\right)$ = _____
5. −0.74 ÷ (−0.17) = _____
6. $\frac{3}{14} \times -\left(\frac{2}{7}\right)$ = _____
7. 1.8 × (−4.5) = _____
8. $-9\frac{1}{2} \times 3\frac{1}{5}$ = _____
9. $-\frac{5}{6} \div \left(-\frac{7}{8}\right)$ = _____
10. $-\frac{4}{5} \times \left(-\frac{9}{10}\right)$ = _____
11. 1.782 × (−2) = _____
12. $-4\frac{2}{7} \div \left(-3\frac{3}{14}\right)$ = _____

Verb tense shows when an action takes place. Write the past tense and past participle of each present-tense verb. Then, use a dictionary to check your work.

	Present	Past	Past Participle
13.	forget	_____	_____
14.	teach	_____	_____
15.	sink	_____	_____
16.	break	_____	_____
17.	freeze	_____	_____
18.	throw	_____	_____
19.	choose	_____	_____
20.	hear	_____	_____

FITNESS FLASH: Do 10 shoulder shrugs.

* See page ii.

DAY 19

Reading Comprehension

Read the passage. Then, answer the questions.

The Blarney Stone

Each year, thousands of tourists visit Blarney Castle in Blarney, Ireland. They come to see, and sometimes kiss, the Blarney Stone, located high in the castle's battlements. The three-story castle was built in 1446 by the King of Munster. The stone that exists today is thought to be half of the original Stone of Scone, which belonged to Scotland. Scottish kings were crowned over the stone because of its alleged magical powers.

How the Blarney Stone earned these alleged powers is unclear. One legend says that an old woman cast a spell on the stone to reward a king for saving her from drowning. Kissing the stone gave the king blarney, which is the ability to speak convincingly.

The term *blarney* may have originated from the many unfulfilled promises of Cormac McCarthy, King of Munster, who promised to give his castle to the Queen of England. But he delayed doing so with soft words, which Queen Elizabeth I described as "blarney talk." Other legends say that the definition came from another king who once lived in the castle. He had the ability to remain in the middle of an argument without taking sides.

Tourists who want to kiss the Blarney Stone do so with great difficulty. They have to lie on their backs and bend backward and down, holding iron bars for support.

21. What is the setting for this passage?
    A. Scotland   B. London   C. Ireland   D. Wales

22. Which of the following best defines the word *blarney*?
    A. understandable conversation   B. confusing speech
    C. skillful flattery or deception   D. nonstop chattering

23. Why do tourists want to kiss the Blarney Stone? _____

24. Do you think that only people who believe in magic will kiss the stone? Why or why not? _____

Problem Solving/Language Arts

DAY 20

Write and solve an equation for each problem.

1. Melissa sold 18 raffle tickets for the school fundraiser. Jonah sold half as many tickets as Melissa. Shona sold 1½ times as many tickets as Melissa. If each ticket cost $6, how much total money did the students raise?

   equation: _____

   answer: _____

2. Tamara is going with her class on a three-day field trip. The cost of the trip is $76 per student. The price includes $14 per night for 2 nights in a hotel. Tamara will also receive 6 meal tickets. Each meal ticket costs the same amount. How much does each meal ticket cost?

   equation: _____

   answer: _____

An *allusion* is a reference to a person, place, or thing from literature, mythology, or history. Find and underline the allusion in each sentence. On the line that follows, explain what the allusion refers to.

3. Jacob looked like Oliver Twist, standing there asking for something else to eat.

   _____

4. Everything looked so strange to Malia when she came home from summer camp. She felt like Alice falling down the rabbit hole.

   _____

5. It's been raining for so long, Dad was just about ready to build an ark!

   _____

6. "No one's perfect," said Mom. "Everyone has an Achilles' heel."

   _____

7. I spent the afternoon scrubbing the house like Cinderella, and Mom still wouldn't let me go to the school dance!

   _____

8. Edward is such a Scrooge—he absolutely hates to part with his money.

   _____

DAY 20

Literary Terms/Writing

A nonfiction report should be free of bias or personal opinion. Elements of bias may include loaded words, generalizations, and stereotypes. Read the following essay about selecting a pet and underline the elements of bias.

Best Pet

When selecting a family pet, consider getting a turtle. A turtle is the perfect pet for everyone. A turtle needs only a little bit of food each day and, with the proper care, can be a fantastic addition to every home. If you handle a turtle, though, be sure to wash your hands thoroughly afterward. Turtles may carry bacteria called *salmonella*, which is dangerous to humans.

Granted, all turtles are lazy, as they sit on their rocks in the sun and do not do much else. But, you can sit in a chair and watch them in your free time. Unlike dogs or cats, which are cute and frisky, turtles are sluggish, but still fascinating.

You will need to provide proper food and housing for your turtle. Give it a large tank so that it has plenty of room to roam. Proper lighting is important as well, so you will have to purchase a special ultraviolet lightbulb. Finally, do not forget to name your new pet.

Think of an advertisement you have recently seen or heard. Describe how the advertisement encouraged consumers to buy a company's product. How did the company convey that its product is the best? Should consumers trust all of the information the advertisement provided? Where might you gather more information about the product to make an informed purchase? Use another piece of paper if you need more space.

_____
_____
_____
_____
_____
_____
_____

CHARACTER CHECK: What is compassion? Make a list of five ways that you can show compassion to your friends, family, animals, and the environment.

Science Experiment

BONUS

Resting and Active Pulse Rates

How does exercise affect your heart rate?

Each time the ventricles of your heart contract, blood is forced into your arteries. Each beat of your heart makes your arteries stretch, which causes the pulsing sensation that you feel. As blood is pushed out of your heart with great force, it moves quickly so that it can reach the parts of your body farthest from your heart.

In this activity, you will find your pulse rate and calculate the number of times that your heart beats per minute. Then, you will determine how exercise affects your heart rate.

Materials:
- paper
- chair
- pencil
- stopwatch

Procedure:
1. Sit in a chair and relax for 1 minute. Use your index and middle fingers to locate your pulse on your wrist or neck.
2. Count the number of beats that you feel in 15 seconds. Multiply this number by 4. This is your resting pulse rate for 1 minute. Record this number in the Resting Pulse Rate column.
3. Jog in place for 1 minute. Then, stop jogging and use your index and middle fingers to locate your pulse on your wrist or neck. Calculate your pulse rate as you did in step 2. Record this number in the Active Pulse Rate column.
4. Repeat steps 1 through 3 two additional times. Then, calculate your average resting and active pulse rates by adding the three trials in each column and dividing by 3.

Trial	Resting Pulse Rate	Active Pulse Rate
1		
2		
3		
Average		

5. Ask some friends to find their resting and active pulse rates, too. Write their average resting and active pulse rates in the correct columns. Then, calculate the average pulse rates for your friends. Do boys and girls have the same or different average pulse rates? How can you explain this?

* See page ii.

Science Experiment

BONUS

Bird Adaptations

How do birds adapt to their environments?

Birds develop different physical features that help them survive. The size and shape of a bird's beak is specific to what it eats. A short, wide beak is usually better for breaking open nuts and seeds. A long, thin beak is better suited to digging for insects and worms. Some birds have longer legs for standing in deep water and catching fish and other water creatures. Other **adaptations** include size, wingspan, foot type, and feather shape.

In this activity, you will create a model of a bird that is physically adapted to live in a specific habitat.

Materials:
- different colors of clay
- cotton swabs
- buttons
- scissors
- feathers
- drinking straws
- twigs
- glue or glue stick
- construction paper
- chenille stems
- small pebbles

Procedure:
1. Choose one of these habitats.
   A. dry, sandy desert with very little water or plant life
   B. cold, mountainous area; very high elevation
   C. Antarctic region where snow and ice cover the ground year-round
   D. tropical rain forest; full of colorful plant life
2. Use the materials to create a model of a bird that is physically adapted to survive in your chosen habitat.
3. Describe the bird's physical adaptations. _____
   _____
   _____
4. How might this bird species adapt if humans or nature changed its habitat?
   _____
   _____
   _____
5. What does the word *adaptation* mean as it is used in this experiment?
   _____

Social Studies Activity

BONUS

Using Latitude and Longitude

Lines of latitude are imaginary lines on a globe or a map used to measure distances north and south of the equator (0°). They are called *parallels* because they are parallel to the equator. Latitude is written as degrees north or south of the equator. Lines of longitude are imaginary lines on a globe or a map used to measure distances east and west of the prime meridian (0°). Lines of longitude are also known as *meridians*, and they run from the north pole to the south pole. Longitude is written as degrees east or west of the prime meridian.

Use an atlas to find the major city located near each coordinate. Each coordinate is rounded to the nearest degree. Then, write the name of the city on the line.

	City	Latitude	Longitude
1.	_____	22°N	114°E
2.	_____	52°N	1°W
3.	_____	34°N	84°W
4.	_____	56°N	3°W
5.	_____	29°N	77°E
6.	_____	26°S	28°E
7.	_____	41°N	2°E
8.	_____	51°N	114°W
9.	_____	38°N	122°W
10.	_____	24°S	47°W

Use an atlas to plot each city. Then, record the latitude and the longitude on the chart, rounding to the nearest degree.

	City	Latitude	Longitude		City	Latitude	Longitude
11.	Paris	_____	_____	12.	Vancouver	_____	_____
13.	Beijing	_____	_____	14.	Athens	_____	_____
15.	Lima	_____	_____	16.	Boston	_____	_____
17.	Honolulu	_____	_____	18.	Mexico City	_____	_____
19.	Venice	_____	_____	20.	Moscow	_____	_____

© Carson Dellosa Education

Forms of Government

Many different types of governments exist in the world. Some examples are listed below. Choose three types of governments from the list. Then, with an adult's permission, go online or visit a library to research the three types. Write a brief description of each government.

communism	emirate	parliamentary democracy
constitutional democracy	federal (federation)	parliamentary monarchy
constitutional monarchy	federal republic	republic
democracy	Islamic republic	socialism
democratic republic	monarchy	theocracy
dictatorship	oligarchy	

1. _____

2. _____

3. _____

Social Studies Activity

BONUS

The Panama Canal

Read the passage. Then, create a time line showing how the Panama Canal was built and changed.

The Panama Canal crosses the Isthmus of Panama and connects the Atlantic and Pacific Oceans. Early travelers had no choice but to sail around South America to get from one ocean to the other. The idea of building a canal across Panama originated during the early 16th century, but the necessary technology had not yet been developed. In 1880, a French company bought the rights to build the canal and began to dig. However, the land was difficult to clear, and many workers suffered from malaria or yellow fever. Work on the canal came to a halt in 1889. Then, in 1903, the United States bought the rights to build and operate the canal. The project was completed on August 5, 1914.

Because of the difficult land and the great distance that the canal covers, some consider it the greatest modern-age engineering creation. The canal stretches for 50 miles (82 km) from deep water in the Atlantic Ocean to deep water in the Pacific Ocean. Its width varies between 500 to 1,000 feet (150 to 300 m), and its depth is at least 41 feet (12.5 m). The canal uses sets of locks that raise and lower passing ships to the proper level for each ocean. It takes a vessel about 15 to 20 hours to cross from one ocean to the other, including waiting time.

In 1977, U.S. President Jimmy Carter signed the Torrijos-Carter Treaty. This treaty, effective December 31, 1999, began the process of handing over control of the canal to Panama. Since that time, the canal has continued to be a great success. However, the development of wider ships has created problems for when they try to pass through the canal. Work to widen and deepen the canal began in 2007.

BONUS

Outdoor Extension Activities

Take It Outside!

Plan a day trip with your family. Bring a pen, a notebook, and a camera. Every hour on the hour, take a picture of where you are. Make a note of the time and location of each picture. After the trip, print the pictures. Make a time line of the day, using hours as your time measurement. Place the pictures on the time line at their appropriate hours. Share your time line with friends and show them the hourly highlights of your family's day trip.

Find an outdoor movie night or community theater presentation in your area. With a family member, select a movie or performance to attend. Bring a pen and a notebook. If you are watching a live performance, read about the play, director, and actors in the printed program. Take notes about your experience during the show or performance. Afterward, read your notes and write a review of the movie or show. Share your review with family members who attended.

Take a walk around your neighborhood. Bring a pen and a notebook with you. Periodically pause and write notes, indicating what you've done, seen, and heard. After the walk, read your notes. Then, write a 50-word summary of your walk. Edit your summary to 30 words. Be sure to keep the key ideas. Can you edit your piece to a 10-word summary?

Choose something you saw on your walk that you'd like to learn more about. It might be a bird, a type of tree, an insect, a style of architecture, or a poster for an upcoming play. Conduct some research about your topic, either online or at the library. Then, write a short essay detailing what you learned from your research. Share your writing with a friend or family member.

* See page ii.

SECTION II

Monthly Goals

Think of three goals to set for yourself this month. For example, you may want to read for 30 minutes each day. Write your goals on the lines. Post them somewhere that you will see them every day.

Draw a check mark beside each goal you meet. Feel proud that you have met your goals and continue to set new ones to challenge yourself.

1. _____
2. _____
3. _____

Word List

The following words are used in this section. Use a dictionary to look up each word that you do not know. Then, write three sentences. Use at least one word from the word list in each sentence.

deficit
extract
gullible
implement
indigenous

innovations
mechanism
metropolitan
pamphlets
segregated

1. _____
_____
2. _____
_____
3. _____
_____

SECTION II

Introduction to Strength

This section includes fitness and character development activities that focus on strength. These activities are designed to get you moving and thinking about strengthening your body and your character.

Physical Strength

Like flexibility, strength is important for a healthy body. Many people think that a strong person is someone who can lift an enormous amount of weight. However, strength is more than the ability to pick up heavy barbells. Having strength is important for many everyday activities, such as helping with yardwork or helping a younger sibling get into a car. Muscular strength also helps reduce stress on your joints as your body ages.

Everyday activities and many fun exercises provide opportunities for you to build strength. Carrying bags of groceries, riding a bicycle, and swimming are all excellent ways to strengthen your muscles. Classic exercises, such as push-ups and chin-ups, are also fantastic strength-builders.

Set realistic, achievable goals to improve your strength based on the activities that you enjoy. Evaluate your progress during the summer months and set new strength goals for yourself as you accomplish your previous goals.

Strength of Character

As you build your physical strength, work on your inner strength as well. Having a strong character means standing up for your beliefs, even if others do not agree with your viewpoint. Inner strength can be shown in many ways. For example, you can show inner strength by being honest, standing up for someone who needs your help, and putting your best effort into every task. It is not always easy to show inner strength. Think of a time when you showed inner strength, such as telling the truth when you broke your mother's favorite vase. How did you use your inner strength to handle that situation?

Use the summer months to develop a strong sense of self, both physically and emotionally. Celebrate your successes and look for ways to become even stronger. Reflect upon your accomplishments during the summer, and you will see positive growth on the inside and on the outside.

Algebra/Grammar

DAY 1

Simplify each expression.

1. $-n + 9n + 3 - 8 - 8n$ _____
2. $4(x + 9y) - 2(2x + 4y)$ _____
3. $3(-4x + 5y) - 3x(2 + 4y)$ _____
4. $4(x + 5y) + (5x + y)$ _____
5. $5 - 4y + x + 9y$ _____
6. $6x + -2y^2 + 4xy^2 + 3x^2 + 5xy^2$ _____
7. $-2x + 3y - 5x - (-8y) + 9y$ _____
8. $-2(c - d) + (c - 3d) - 5(c - d)$ _____
9. $6(a - b) - 5(2a + 4b)$ _____
10. $3x + (-3y) - (4x) + y$ _____
11. $7(x + 5y) + 3(x + 5y) + 5(3x + 8y)$
12. $-3(4x + -2y) - 2(x + 3y) - 2(2x + 6y)$
13. $12x + 6x + 9x - 3y + (-7y) + y$ _____
14. $2b + 3(2b + 8z) - 3(8b + 2a)$ _____
15. $-21x + (-2x)$ _____
16. $3[2(-y^2 + y) - 3] - 3(2x + y)$ _____

A *modifier* is a word or group of words that describe a noun or pronoun. In sentences with a *dangling modifier*, it is unclear what the modifier is describing. Each sentence contains a dangling modifier. Rewrite it to make clear what the modifier is describing.

EXAMPLE: While walking to school, a barking dog chased after me.
While I was walking to school, a barking dog chased after me.

17. While studying for a history test, Dad called me down for dinner.
   _____

18. Practicing piano after dinner, my sister said I was really improving.
   _____

19. Walking the trail at the park, the birds sang cheerfully.
   _____

20. After rehearsing my lines for the play, Mom said she thought I'd do very well on opening night.
   _____

21. Though he was not very athletic, Darren taught Micah to play football.
   _____

DAY 1

Vocabulary/Science

Read each word. Write *P* if the word has a positive connotation and *N* if the word has a negative connotation.

22. _____ absurd
23. _____ intrepid
24. _____ radiant
25. _____ assertive
26. _____ thrifty
27. _____ sabotage
28. _____ arrogant
29. _____ obsolete

Write the word from the word bank that matches each description.

| diffuse reflection | reflection | opaque | lens | focal point |
| ray | translucent | convex | transparent | concave |

30. _____ a material that allows some light to pass through
31. _____ a material that absorbs or reflects light
32. _____ when light rays hit a rough surface and bounce back at different angles
33. _____ a straight line that represents a light wave
34. _____ when light rays hit a smooth surface and bounce back at the same angle
35. _____ curved outward
36. _____ a curved piece of glass used to refract light
37. _____ a material that allows most light to pass through
38. _____ the point where light waves appear to meet after being reflected by a mirror or lens
39. _____ curved inward

FACTOID: Breakfast cereal was invented in 1863 by James Caleb Jackson.

Algebra/Parts of Speech

DAY 2

Complete each equation.

1. $a + 3a = 1a + 3a = (1 + \underline{})\, a$
2. $(6t + 5t) = \underline{}(6 + 5)$

Rewrite each expression using the distributive property. Do not simplify.

3. $4(12 + 15)$ _____
4. $3a + 6b$ _____
5. $(10 + 13)t$ _____
6. $x(6 + 8)$ _____
7. $7r + 8r + 2$ _____
8. $2(5x + 8y)$ _____

Use the distributive property to simplify each expression.

9. $7a + a + 15$ _____
10. $k + 5 + 7 + 3k$ _____
11. $2(b + 4) + 8b$ _____
12. $2c + 6c + 9(c + 3)$ _____

Circle the complete verb in each sentence. Then, write *present progressive*, *past progressive*, *future progressive*, *present perfect*, or *future perfect* to describe the verb tense in the sentence.

13. _____ Anna Mason is running for seventh-grade student council representative.
14. _____ Matthew was staying after work for a good reason.
15. _____ My uncle had told his story many times before.
16. _____ The director of marketing will be approving this ad.
17. _____ Larry and Lee have played golf together for years.
18. _____ The trees in our backyard were swaying back and forth during the recent storm.
19. _____ The reporter will be interviewing the eyewitness.

DAY 2

Reading Comprehension

Read the passage. Then, answer the questions.

The Silk Road

The Silk Road was not really a road, nor was it made of silk. The Silk Road refers to a network of trade routes leading from Asia to the West. Many people, including Italian adventurer Marco Polo, traveled along these routes. They often traded goods, such as silk and spices from China, and gold and silver from Italy. However, few people traveled the entire distance of the Silk Road because it was several thousand miles long and very dangerous. The routes covered challenging terrain, such as deserts and mountains, and there was always the danger of meeting bandits. People traded with each other along the way and took goods with them to others farther along the route. In addition to goods, people also traded ideas and inventions along the Silk Road. Travelers even brought such technological innovations as the magnetic compass from Asia to the West.

20. What is the main idea of this passage?
    A. Many people traded goods and ideas along the Silk Road.
    B. The Silk Road was long and dangerous.
    C. Marco Polo traveled along the Silk Road.

21. What was the Silk Road? _____
    _____

22. What did people trade along the Silk Road? _____
    _____

23. Why did few people travel the entire distance of the Silk Road? _____
    _____

24. Write one technological innovation that was brought from Asia to the West.
    _____

FITNESS FLASH: Do five push-ups.

* See page ii.

Algebra/Vocabulary

DAY 3

Find the value of each variable.

1. $3x - 23 = 13$
2. $5t + 3 = 18$
3. $6 + 3m = -12$

4. $7k - 56 = -7$
5. $-32 = -6s + 4$
6. $7 + \frac{1}{4}r = -17$

7. $101 = 14 + 3d$
8. $-25 = \frac{1}{5}h + 5$
9. $8 = -2c + 24$

10. $\frac{1}{2}j + 4 = -15$
11. $2p - 5 = -5$
12. $-16 = 12z - 100$

In sentences marked with S, underline two words that are synonyms. In sentences marked with A, underline two words that are antonyms.

13. (S) The gray weather added to Alessandro's melancholy mood, but he knew he would feel less depressed once the sun returned.
14. (A) Although Kia and Kellan are twins, Kia is an introverted person, while Kellan is quite sociable.
15. (S) When power went off at the restaurant, the owner tried to placate the irritated customers, but nothing seemed to appease them.
16. (A) Mrs. Kent asked the instructor whether the test was compulsory or voluntary.
17. (A) When you conduct the experiment, what response do you expect the stimulus to create?
18. (S) "I'll need to see a valid driver's license or some other legitimate form of ID," the ticket agent told Dad.
19. (A) We planned to carefully cultivate the garden this summer, but we managed to neglect it after only a few weeks.

DAY 3

Vocabulary/Algebra

Read each sentence. Circle the correct meaning of the underlined word as it is used in the sentence.

20. The farmer made <u>furrows</u> in the earth with the plow.
    A. deep troughs to plant crops in B. wrinkles in a person's brow

21. My teacher asked me to <u>condense</u> my report to one page.
    A. change from vapor to liquid B. make shorter or more compact

22. I <u>skimmed</u> the material one more time before the test.
    A. looked at quickly B. glided across

23. We were asked to <u>refrain</u> from talking during the assembly.
    A. avoid B. repeated part of a song

24. The city's new development <u>sprawls</u> over many miles.
    A. lies down B. stretches out

Simplify each problem.

25. $|-12|$ _____

26. $-|10|$ _____

27. $|0|$ _____

28. $|-13| + |-12|$ _____

29. $|-14| - |5|$ _____

30. $-|-15|$ _____

FACTOID: Earth is 7,926 miles (12,756 km) in diameter.

Writing/Grammar

DAY 4

Use the Internet to research making compost for a garden. Find different methods used to make compost. Write a paragraph to explain each method. Use a strong topic sentence and supporting details in each paragraph. Use a separate sheet of paper if you need more space.

_____
_____
_____
_____
_____
_____
_____
_____
_____
_____

A *compound-complex sentence* contains two or more independent clauses and one or more dependent clauses. In each sentence, circle the independent clauses. Underline the dependent clause.

1. Even though they were exhausted from their long day, the seventh graders held a dance that night, and the eighth graders saw a play.

2. Isaac Newton described the relationship between force, mass, and acceleration, and he made discoveries in optics and mathematics, to name just a few of his contributions to science.

3. Nikki has learned some computer coding, but she also wants to study graphic design, which is being taught at the community center this winter.

4. After a huge victory last week, the Jayhawks are a favorite in today's game, so a trip to the playoffs could be in their future.

FITNESS FLASH: Do five push-ups.

* See page ii.

DAY 4

Match each root word in the first column with its meaning in the second column. Use a dictionary if you need help.

meter as in thermometer	large, powerful
scope as in stethoscope	measure
struct as in construction	angle
dict as in dictation	stars, space
astro as in astronomer	time
mega as in megaphone	little, tiny
chron as in chronology	view
min as in miniscule	build
gon as in polygon	speak

Plank Practice

Strong muscles and bones are important for fitness and overall health. Strengthen your arms, back, wrists, and abdomen with the yoga plank pose.

While it may seem easy, this yoga pose can be very challenging, so start slowly. Begin by lying on your stomach. Place your hands by your shoulders with your palms flat on the floor. Lift yourself into a push-up position. Align your head and neck with your back and keep your back flat. Your shoulders should be directly above your elbows. Now, tighten your abdomen. If this is too difficult, lower your knees to the floor. Remember to breathe. Hold the pose for 10 seconds. Then, slowly lower yourself to the starting position. Repeat this activity two or three times.

FITNESS FLASH: Do 10 lunges.

*See page ii.

Measurement/Grammar

DAY 5

Find the area and perimeter of each polygon. Show your work on a separate sheet of paper.

1.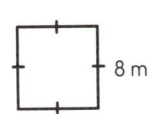

   A= _____ P= _____

2.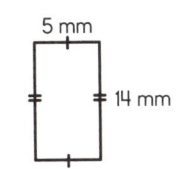

   A= _____ P= _____

3.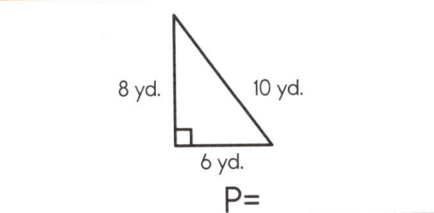

   A= _____ P= _____

4.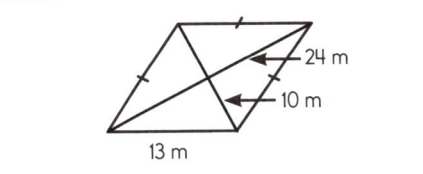

   A= _____ P= _____

5.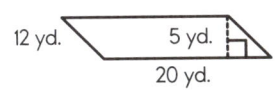

   A= _____ P= _____

6.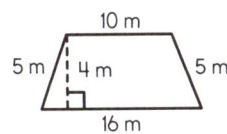

   A= _____ P= _____

Underline the subject(s) of each sentence. Then, circle the verb that correctly completes each sentence.

7. Kiley (brings, bring) her pet lizard to school every year for "Pets on Parade Week."

8. Gretchen (goes, go) home every weekend to see her parents.

9. Carlos and Ben (has been, have been) friends since third grade.

10. A statue of Andrew Jackson (stands, stand) in the middle of Jackson Square in New Orleans, Louisiana.

11. Two professional baseball teams (calls, call) New York City their home.

12. Trail Ridge Road (winds, wind) its way through Rocky Mountain National Park.

13. The questions (was, were) difficult for the candidate.

14. The president and vice president (runs, run) as a team while in a presidential election.

DAY 5

Reading Comprehension

Read the passage. Then, answer the questions.

Jackie Robinson (1919–1972)

Jackie Robinson's interest in sports began early in his life. He attended college at UCLA and lettered in baseball, basketball, football, and track. When Robinson, who was an African American player, was growing up, sports teams were **segregated**. Black athletes and white athletes could not play together. Only white players were allowed to be on professional sports teams.

Jackie Robinson pioneered racial integration in professional sports. In 1947, he joined the Brooklyn Dodgers, a baseball team in New York. Many fans were angry that an African American was on the team. Some wrote threatening letters; others mocked Robinson on the field. Some players did not want him on the team. But, he did not give up; he kept playing. He did so well his first season that he was named Rookie of the Year.

In the 10 years that Jackie Robinson played for the Dodgers, the team won six National League pennants and played in the World Series. Robinson retired in 1956, later raising money for the National Association for the Advancement of Colored People (NAACP) and speaking for the rights of African Americans. He also was elected to the Baseball Hall of Fame. Robinson broke the color barrier in major league baseball, which opened the sports world to other African American players.

15. Choose a good title for this passage.
    A. Breaking the Color Barrier in Sports
    B. A Great Baseball Player
    C. Jackie Robinson's College Years
    D. Rookie of the Year

16. What does the word *segregated* mean in the story?
    A. forced to play together
    B. divided into teams
    C. kept apart by race
    D. mixed together

17. What is the purpose of the second paragraph in the passage? How does the author support that purpose? _____

_____

18. Why was Robinson's baseball career important? _____

_____

CHARACTER CHECK: Make a list of five things you can do at home that demonstrate cooperation. Post the list and invite family members to add to it.

Measurement/Language Arts

DAY 6

Find the volume of each solid. Round to the nearest hundredth. Show your work on a separate sheet of paper.

1.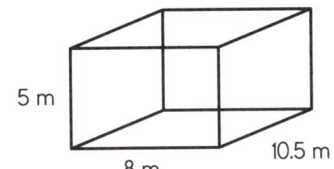

   V = _____

2.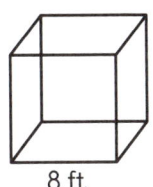

   V = _____

3.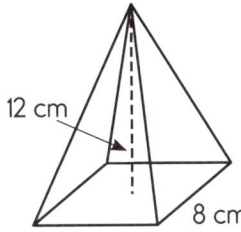

   V = _____

4.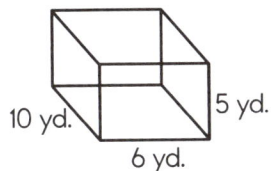

   V = _____

5.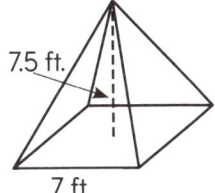

   V = _____

6.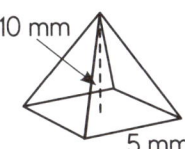

   V = _____

Circle the letter of the misspelled word in each row. Write the correct spelling on the line.

7.	A.	agile	B.	dwindel	C.	biscuit	_____
8.	A.	mildew	B.	forfiet	C.	gorgeous	_____
9.	A.	surgeon	B.	caustic	C.	asteriks	_____
10.	A.	emphasize	B.	rigerous	C.	conjugate	_____
11.	A.	specimen	B.	forage	C.	aquaint	_____
12.	A.	dismall	B.	amnesty	C.	succumb	_____
13.	A.	centenial	B.	accomplice	C.	exhaust	_____
14.	A.	suburban	B.	analagy	C.	cafeteria	_____
15.	A.	occasion	B.	strength	C.	redundent	_____
16.	A.	austeer	B.	embellish	C.	precaution	_____
17.	A.	eficient	B.	notorious	C.	acquire	_____
18.	A.	concede	B.	legible	C.	capasity	_____

DAY 6

Vocabulary/Writing

Circle the word that correctly completes each analogy.

19. Stiff is to flexible as empty is to _____.
    A. low B. rigid
    C. full D. elastic

20. Glass is to transparent as wood is to _____.
    A. clear B. opaque
    C. pine D. fragile

21. Waltz is to dance as oak is to _____.
    A. acorn B. tree
    C. pine D. tango

22. Laugh is to tickle as shiver is to _____.
    A. cold B. bored
    C. giggle D. amused

23. Star is to galaxy as word is to _____.
    A. universe B. alphabet
    C. planet D. dictionary

24. Thrifty is to cheap as smart is to _____.
    A. dull B. foolish
    C. gullible D. brilliant

25. A chapter is to a book as an act is to a _____.
    A. novel B. comedy
    C. play D. sitcom

26. Precise is to exact as lively is to _____.
    A. energetic B. listless
    C. inaccurate D. quick

Write about ways that daily life has changed in the last century because of technology. Use specific details and examples to explain how these technological advances have changed daily life.

_____
_____
_____
_____
_____
_____

Algebra & Ratios

DAY 7

Solve each proportion. Use cross products.

1. $\dfrac{1}{4} = \dfrac{x}{8}$
2. $\dfrac{20}{30} = \dfrac{5}{d}$
3. $\dfrac{18}{24} = \dfrac{12}{l}$
4. $\dfrac{80}{m} = \dfrac{48}{20}$

5. $\dfrac{5}{5} = \dfrac{5n}{5}$
6. $\dfrac{15}{45} = \dfrac{3}{t}$
7. $\dfrac{1.8}{v} = \dfrac{3.6}{2.8}$
8. $\dfrac{8}{z} = \dfrac{5}{2}$

9. $\dfrac{8}{6} = \dfrac{s}{27}$
10. $\dfrac{144}{6} = \dfrac{6c}{6}$
11. $\dfrac{r}{3} = \dfrac{8}{8}$
12. $\dfrac{36}{12} = \dfrac{b}{6}$

13. $\dfrac{0.14}{0.07} = \dfrac{k}{1.5}$
14. $\dfrac{6}{w} = \dfrac{6}{4}$
15. $\dfrac{4}{5} = \dfrac{f}{5}$
16. $\dfrac{16}{48} = \dfrac{h}{50}$

Solve each inequality and graph its solution.

17. $15 \times x \leq 15$

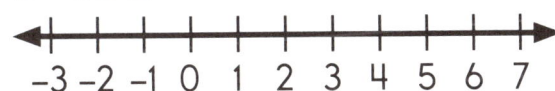

18. $h \div 6 < -12$

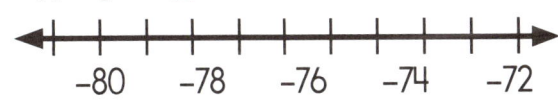

19. $-10a < -70$

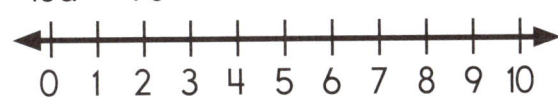

20. $n \div 2 \geq 2$

DAY 7

Data Analysis/Critical Thinking

Compare the two sets of data. For each, examine the distribution and find the measures of center. Then, write several sentences that compare the sets.

Number of Books Read Over the Summer	
Homeroom A	Homeroom B
5, 9, 10, 15, 4, 3, 0, 9, 6, 7, 1, 2, 5, 10	6, 5, 7, 4, 8, 9, 9, 5, 10, 12, 15, 3, 0, 6

_____
_____
_____
_____
_____

Read the first word pair. Make the next word pair by taking the second word from the previous word pair and combining it with a word from the word bank. Word pairs must combine to form either a compound word or words that are often used together. The goal is to reach the last word pair provided.

ball	dragon	finger	fly	snap
dragon	finger	fly	ring	snap

21. key, ring
22. _____
23. _____
24. _____
25. _____
26. _____
27. ball, game

FITNESS FLASH: Do 10 sit-ups.

* See page ii.

Problem Solving/Grammar

DAY 8

Solve each problem. Round each answer to two decimal places.

1. If 3 square feet of fabric costs $3.75, what would 7 square feet cost?

2. A 12-ounce bottle of soap costs $2.50. How many ounces would be in a bottle that costs $3.75?

3. Four pounds of apples cost $5.00. How much would 10 pounds of apples cost?

4. A 12-ounce can of lemonade costs $1.32. How much would a 16-ounce can of lemonade cost?

5. A 32-pound box of cantaloupes costs $24.40. How much would a 12-pound box cost?

6. If a 10-pound turkey costs $20.42, how much does a 21-pound turkey cost?

Varying the lengths of your sentences will help maintain your reader's attention. Combine each sentence pair into a single sentence that retains all of the important information.

7. Kelly worked for years as a consultant for Harnquist and Beckman. She now has her own consulting firm. _____

8. Lake Powell occupies parts of both Arizona and Utah. It is the largest lake in either state. _____

9. We had box seats in the front row. We could put our drinks on top of the Cardinal's dugout. _____

DAY 8

Reading Comprehension

Read the passage. Then, answer the questions.

What's in a Coral Reef?

A coral reef is like a complex city that supports a dazzling array of life almost as diverse as that of a rain forest. The architects of these underwater habitats are animals called *coral polyps*. Usually no bigger than peas, coral polyps look like tiny, colorful flowers.

Coral polyps extract calcium from seawater and convert it to limestone. The limestone forms little cups of rock to support their soft bodies. Each polyp attaches to its neighbor with the skeleton formed by its outer skin, forming coral colonies. As polyps grow, they build new cup skeletons on top of old ones. Limestone formations built by millions of coral polyps are called *coral reefs*. Structures formed by the polyps may be branches, cups, ripples, discs, fans, or columns. Each kind of coral grows in a specific pattern.

Densely populated coral reefs provide habitats for an amazing **diversity** of marine life, including neon-colored fish, moray eels, soft corals, sponges, tube worms, barracuda, sharks, starfish, manta rays, sea turtles, lobsters, crabs, and shrimp.

Coral fossils indicate that coral reefs have existed for millions of years. The solid appearance of reefs might lead us to think that they are permanent. However, coral reefs are fragile, carefully balanced ecosystems that are easily threatened. A change in the temperature, water quality, or light can kill the coral polyps.

Some destruction of coral reefs may result from these natural causes, but humans cause the greatest damage to reefs. Once a reef is damaged, it may never recover, and the entire coral community may be lost.

10. Why are coral reefs described as complex cities? _____

_____

11. Which of the following best defines the word *diversity*?
    A. a home for marine animals   B. a variety
    C. a school of brightly colored fish   D. a specific pattern

12. The diversity of coral reefs is second only to the diversity found in _____ .

13. Why do polyps extract calcium from seawater? _____

14. Based on the selection, what is the author's point of view on coral reefs?

_____

15. What distinction does the author make between the solid appearance of coral reefs and their actual status? _____

Percentages/Parts of Speech

DAY 9

Write a proportion to represent each problem. Solve the proportion.

1. 45 is what percentage of 90? _____
2. What percentage of 100 is 19? _____
3. What is 75% of 60? _____
4. 35% is 7 out of what number? _____
5. 62% of what number is 9.5? _____
6. 60% of what number is 50.4? _____
7. 7 out of 28 is what percentage? _____
8. 90 is 100% of what number? _____
9. How much is 72% of 54? _____
10. What percentage of 132 is 76.56? _____

Identify the part of speech that describes each underlined word. Write *P* for pronoun or *A* for adjective.

11. _____ This is my best friend.
12. _____ Bruce will buy whichever is left.
13. _____ Emma can buy any book she wants.
14. _____ Was Bob interested in them?
15. _____ This is my favorite flavor of ice cream.
16. _____ Betty ate some of these carrots with dip.
17. _____ Those girls read *Wuthering Heights* this summer.
18. _____ Each found a seat in the theater.
19. _____ Those weren't on the shelf.
20. _____ Cheryl doesn't want any, but McKenna would like a brownie.

FACTOID: Australia's Great Barrier Reef can be seen from outer space.

DAY 9

Vocabulary/Character Development

Read each sentence. Use the context clues to determine the definition of each boldfaced word. Then, write the letter of the correct definition on the line.

21. _____ My **initial** impression was that soccer was a difficult game, but I soon changed my mind.

22. _____ The **narrator** of the documentary spoke in a very soft voice.

23. _____ Volunteers distributed **pamphlets** listing ways that people could help the environment.

24. _____ We will **implement** our new plan next week.

25. _____ I have a strong **hunch** that it will snow tomorrow.

26. _____ Mom is good at **motivating** me to try to do well.

27. _____ Last year, we moved from a rural area to a **metropolitan** region.

28. _____ Candace **excels** at math and science.

A. put into action

B. first, or at the beginning

C. area around and including a city

D. someone speaking

E. inspiring

F. small, printed papers

G. feeling or guess

H. does well

Demonstrating Integrity

Integrity means having sound moral principles and being upstanding, honest, and sincere. Select one of the following situations. Draw two four-panel comic strips to show possible consequences of demonstrating and not demonstrating integrity.

- You are at the movies with friends. While in line at the concession stand, you realize that you do not have enough money to buy everything you want. You notice that a person in front of you has unknowingly dropped a five-dollar bill on the floor.

- You are having fun swimming with your best friend and other good friends from school. Your best friend wants to stay longer, and you really want to stay too. However, you promised to help your grandparents with a project later that day. If you stay at the pool with your friends, you will not be able to help your grandparents.

FITNESS FLASH: Do 10 squats.

* See page ii.

Measurement/Parts of Speech

DAY 10

Find the area and perimeter of each triangle. Show your work on a separate sheet of paper.

1.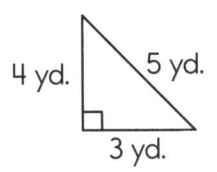

   A=_____ P=_____

2.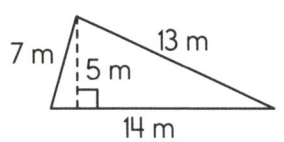

   A=_____ P=_____

3.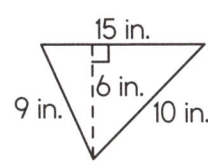

   A=_____ P=_____

4.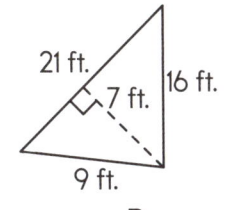

   A=_____ P=_____

5.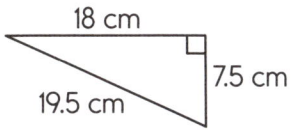

   A=_____ P=_____

6.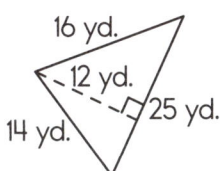

   A=_____ P=_____

7.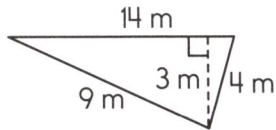

   A=_____ P=_____

8.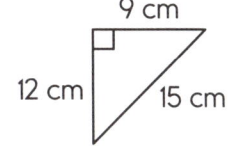

   A=_____ P=_____

9.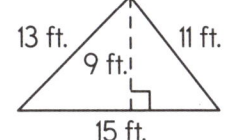

   A=_____ P=_____

A *participle* is a word formed from a verb, which can be used as an adjective. A present participle is formed by adding *-ing*. A past participle is formed by adding *-ed*. Underline the participle in each sentence. On the line, write *PR* if it is a present participle and *PA* if it is a past participle.

EXAMPLE: __PA__ After cooking the garlic, place the chopped carrots in the pan.
          __PR__ Kyle went to see what his giggling cousins were up to.

10. _____ The roller coaster's twisting track rose high over the park.
11. _____ Grandma and I sipped lemonade on the covered porch.
12. _____ The trampled leaves show where a deer rested for the night.
13. _____ My friend Bradley and I invented a jumping game to play on his families trampoline.
14. _____ After the water fight, broken balloons littered the yard.

DAY 10

Vocabulary/Science

Read each sentence. Use the context clues to determine the definition of each boldfaced word. Then, write the letter of the correct definition on the line.

15. _____ Ms. Yang **demonstrated** the experiment.
16. _____ My brother and I **typically** spend each summer at our grandmother's house.
17. _____ The sportscaster **predicted** that the visiting team would win the game.
18. _____ My **schedule** includes activities every day after school.
19. _____ The coach asked us to keep our plans **flexible** in case our team made the play-offs.
20. _____ Eating a variety of foods **nourishes** the body.
21. _____ Mom fixed the **mechanism** so that she could move the garage door up and down.
22. _____ The jury had reached a **verdict**.

A. foretold
B. mechanical device
C. showed how to do
D. changeable
E. provides nutrients for
F. usually
G. decision
H. plans

Write the word from the word bank that matches each description.

| lithosphere | outer core | inner core |
| mantle | atmosphere | crust |

23. _____ layer of molten iron and nickel that surrounds the inner core
24. _____ thinnest, outermost layer of Earth; ranges from about 3 miles (5 km) to 62 miles (100 km) thick
25. _____ layer of hot, solid material between the crust and Earth's core
26. _____ rigid layer consisting of the crust and outermost part of the mantle
27. _____ dense sphere of solid iron and nickel at the center of Earth
28. _____ soft layer of the mantle on which pieces of lithosphere slowly float

CHARACTER CHECK: Look up the word *responsible* in a dictionary. How do you demonstrate responsibility?

Ratios/Literary Terms

DAY 11

A *rational number* can be expressed as a ratio or fraction. When changed to a decimal, its digits end in *0* or repeat. An *irrational number* cannot be expressed as a ratio. When changed into a decimal, its digits go on forever without repeating. Write *R* if the number is rational. Write *I* if the number is irrational.

1. −12 _____
2. 8^2 _____
3. $\frac{3}{7}$ _____
4. $\sqrt{49}$ _____
5. 14.57849 _____
6. $12.3\overline{3}$ _____
7. $\sqrt{2}$ _____
8. −3.22 _____
9. 8.234782649 … _____
10. π _____
11. $\sqrt{144}$ _____
12. $\frac{-4}{5}$ _____

Write the letter of the word from the word bank that matches each description.

A. conflict	B. foreshadowing	C. irony	D. dialogue
E. imagery	F. point of view	G. hyperbole	H. personification
I. setting	J. allusion		

13. _____ the struggle within a story
14. _____ a reference to a person, place, or event
15. _____ spoken conversation between characters
16. _____ exaggeration for effect
17. _____ hints or clues about what might happen later
18. _____ giving human qualities to animals or objects
19. _____ the perspective from which a story is told
20. _____ the time and place in which a story occurs
21. _____ using words that mean the opposite of what one intends
22. _____ descriptive language that forms vivid mental pictures

FITNESS FLASH: Do 10 lunges.

* See page ii.

DAY 11

Reading Comprehension

Read the passage. Then, answer the questions.

Molly Pitcher

Molly ran quickly and carefully through the battlefield, following the empty spaces between wounded soldiers scattered across the ground. As Molly passed the injured men, several reached out in request for water, but her destination was the front lines. She knew that others—including a doctor—would tend to the needs of the fallen soldiers on the battlefield.

Up ahead, through the smoke and dust, Molly could make out the silhouettes of men scrambling to and fro among the cannons. With her pitcher in hand, Molly rushed up to one of the cannons.

"Look out!" a soldier yelled. A British cannonball rocketed across the ground and passed inches from Molly's feet. She hardly flinched as it flew by. She had learned early on to have steady nerves.

As bullets whizzed by, Molly handed the pitcher to the nearest soldier. He drank thirstily, and then the pitcher was handed off to the next man. After the team had drunk their fill, the remaining water was dumped into a bucket. The cannon would need cooling as well.

Suddenly, Molly heard a man call her name. She turned to see that her husband, William, had fallen to the ground. As another soldier tended to him, Molly understood what it meant. Six men were needed to operate a cannon; now they were one short.

Molly didn't hesitate. She had watched men operating cannons for weeks—she knew exactly how they worked—so she jumped in with her husband's team. A female soldier was unheard of, but at that moment, the men hardly gave it a thought. Soon the cannon was firing again, and that was all that mattered.

23. Write two sentences describing Molly's character. _____

24. What is the main idea of the story? _____

25. If this story were told from William's point of view, how would it be different? How would it be the same? _____

© Carson Dellosa Education

Geometry/Parts of Speech

DAY 12

Write the letter of each word next to its definition.

1. _____ two angles with a side and vertex in common
2. _____ pairs of angles that lie outside the parallel lines on opposite sides of the transversal
3. _____ pairs of angles that lie between the parallel lines on opposite sides of the transversal
4. _____ two angles whose measurements equal 180°
5. _____ the amount of space within a three-dimensional figure (measured in cubic units)
6. _____ the sum of the areas of all of the faces of a three-dimensional figure
7. _____ the distance around a two-dimensional, closed figure
8. _____ pairs of angles that appear in corresponding positions in the two sets of angles that were formed by the parallel lines cut by the transversal
9. _____ angles with equivalent measurements
10. _____ two angles whose measurements equal 90°
11. _____ the perimeter of a circle
12. _____ the surface space within a two-dimensional, closed figure (measured in square units)

A. area
B. congruent angles
C. alternate interior angles
D. volume
E. supplementary angles
F. complementary angles
G. adjacent angles
H. alternate exterior angles
I. perimeter
J. surface area
K. circumference
L. corresponding angles

Identify the underlined word in each sentence. Write *ADJ* for adjective and *ADV* for adverb.

13. _____ April answered the questions as accurately as she possibly could.
14. _____ The center, Rex, is the tallest player on our basketball team.
15. _____ Miss Gray's test today was the most difficult one she has given all year.
16. _____ His cousin is a reporter who appears nightly on a local news show.
17. _____ How quickly does our new employee type on his computer?
18. _____ Tonight probably will be a great night to see the meteor shower.
19. _____ Do you think that the World Wide Web was the most useful technological invention of the 20th century?

Reading Comprehension

DAY 12

Read the passage. Then, answer the questions.

The Science of Sleep

Every living creature needs sleep. You may not realize it, but many important things happen to your body and mind during sleep. While you sleep, your heart, lungs, muscles, nervous system, digestive system, and skeletal system rest and prepare for another day. Your body repairs itself during this time. Getting enough sleep also helps your body prevent and fight sickness.

Insufficient sleep results in sleep debt, or an amount of sleep that is owed to your body. Sleep debt affects how you function. People with this deficit may not think that they are sleepy, but they are less able to concentrate or learn new information. They may be irritable, emotional, or have a slower reaction time.

During sleep, your body passes through a five-stage cycle. In the first stage, you are either just beginning to fall asleep or are sleeping lightly. During the second stage, your breathing and heart rate become regular, and your body temperature starts to drop. The third and fourth stages are the deepest, most restful stages of sleep. Throughout these stages, your muscles relax, and your breathing and heart rate become slow and regular. During the fifth and final stage of sleep, your brain gets the critical rest that it needs to function well the next day. During this last stage of sleep, you reach and maintain rapid eye movement (REM), which means that your eyeballs move rapidly under your closed eyelids. REM is also the stage of sleep in which you dream. An entire sleep cycle lasts about 100 minutes and is repeated five or six times every night.

Every individual has his own sleep needs, but researchers have determined that teens need between 8.5 and 9.25 hours of sleep each night to restore full brain function the following day.

20. Write the main idea of the passage. _____
    _____

21. Underline three details in the passage that support the main idea.

22. What is the author's purpose in writing this selection? _____
    _____

23. Based on the selection, do you think the author provides sufficient evidence to support the importance of getting enough sleep? Explain. _____
    _____
    _____
    _____

Multiplication & Division/Grammar

DAY 13

Rewrite each multiplication or division expression using a base and an exponent. Then, evaluate the expression.

1. $6^3 \times 6^{-2} =$ _____ = _____

2. $2^4 \times 2^2 =$ _____ = _____

3. $5^{-3} \div 5^{-6} =$ _____ = _____

4. $3^3 \times 3^2 =$ _____ = _____

5. $7^4 \div 7^5 =$ _____ = _____

6. $10^7 \div 10^4 =$ _____ = _____

7. $10^3 \times 10^5 =$ _____ = _____

8. $6^3 \times 6^{-2} =$ _____ = _____

9. $4^{-5} \div 4^{-8} =$ _____ = _____

10. $8^2 \times 8^2 =$ _____ = _____

11. $11^3 \div 11^5 =$ _____ = _____

12. $2^2 \times 2^{-8} =$ _____ = _____

When the subject of a sentence performs the action, the verb is in the active voice. When the subject of a sentence is being acted upon, the verb is in the passive voice. Rewrite each sentence in the active voice.

13. I was fascinated by the movie *The Sound of Music*. _____

14. The young children in the classroom were amazed by the deputy's words.
_____
_____

15. The toy was chased by Meghan's cat Buffy. _____
_____

16. Lucy was sprayed in the face when she opened the soft drink.
_____
_____

17. A goal was scored by Andy Rahal of the Crosby Middle School soccer team.
_____
_____

DAY 13

Writing/Fitness

When you summarize a story or article, you use your own words to give only the most important information. Write a two-sentence summary of the passage.

Marsha Finds a Pet

All Marsha ever wanted was a pet of her own. On her 13th birthday, Marsha's mother agreed to let her adopt a puppy. They rode the trolley to the local animal shelter. First, Marsha saw a six-month-old cocker spaniel. The puppy was cute, but it was not quite right for her. Then, Marsha saw a golden-haired collie running in circles and trying to catch his tail. "That's the one!" Marsha exclaimed, laughing excitedly and pointing with great satisfaction. Marsha had found the pet of her dreams.

_____

_____

_____

_____

Wall-Sit Challenge

Wall-sits are a great way to increase lower-body strength. Begin by standing with your back about two feet from a wall. Then, while leaning against the wall, slide down, bending your knees until your thighs are parallel to the ground (at about a 90-degree angle). You should feel like you are sitting in an imaginary chair. Hold that position for 10 seconds, and then stand up. Try again, holding the position for as long as you can. As an additional challenge, try raising one leg at a time for a few seconds while holding the position. Set monthly goals to increase the length of time that you stay in a wall-sit and enjoy the benefit of a strong lower body.

FACTOID: Only one percent of the world's water is drinkable.

* See page ii.

Algebra/Grammar

DAY 14

Find several values for *x* and *y* that make each equation true. Use the values to create ordered pairs (*x*, *y*). Then, graph each proportional relationship.

1. $y = 2x$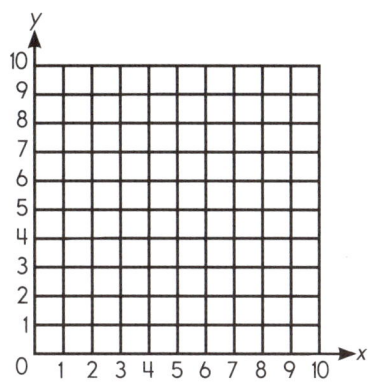

2. $y = \frac{1}{4}x$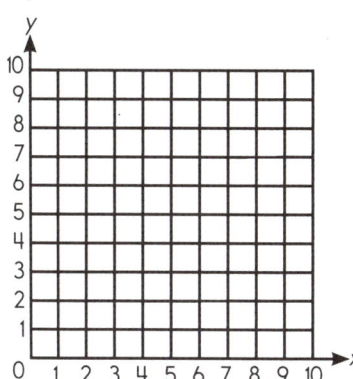

3. $y = 3x$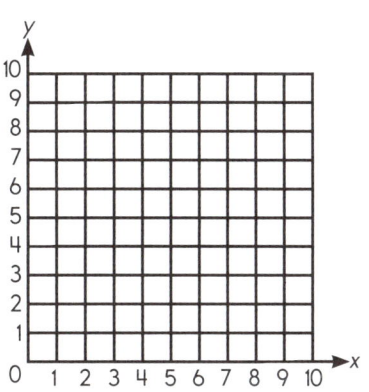

4. $y = \frac{1}{3}x$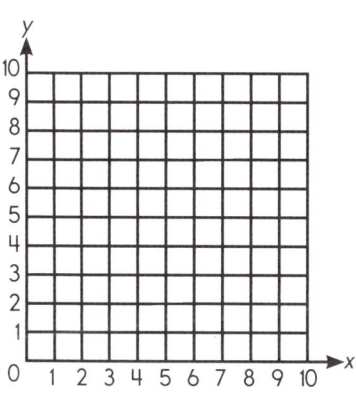

A *prepositional phrase* includes a preposition, its object, and all of the words that modify the object. In each sentence, underline each prepositional phrase and circle its preposition.

5. Audrey left her wallet by the phone in the Louisville, Kentucky, airport.
6. The mayor's wife enjoyed entertaining people who did business with the city.
7. I cannot possibly complete my report without that information.
8. The bird in the tree is a yellow finch.
9. Jonathan saved enough allowance money to go to the movies.
10. Pete brought his expertise to the booth as a member of the new broadcast team.
11. If you are missing any money, check under the cushions of the sofa.
12. The tunnel followed a path under the two buildings.
13. Marc always orders baked ziti at Italian restaurants.

DAY 14

Reading Comprehension

Read the passage. Then, answer the questions.

National Parks

National parks are areas of land set aside to preserve wildlife and to offer places where visitors can experience and enjoy natural settings. Laws protect these parks so that people cannot use them to profit, hunt animals, or damage plants in any way.

In the 1800s, fewer than 10 national parks existed in Canada and the United States. Yellowstone, the first U.S. national park, was established in 1872. Yellowstone covers parts of three states. It is famous for its geysers, hot springs, and scenery. Canada established its first national park in 1885. Banff National Park in Alberta sits in the Rocky Mountains and is known for its mountains, its glaciers, its array of wildlife, and Lake Louise.

Eventually, the idea of national parks caught on internationally during the late 1800s and early 1900s. National parks now protect the world's highest mountains, largest waterfalls, and other important natural features on nearly every continent.

Many national parks experience problems protecting their natural environments. Native animals can reproduce rapidly and overpopulate the areas. The large volume of park visitors can make controlling misuse difficult. The huge size of some parks also makes protected animals easy targets for **poachers**.

Even with these problems, national parks are wonderful places to visit. National parks can help people appreciate nature and learn more about the world.

14. What is the main idea of this passage?
    A. National parks can be found all over the world.
    B. National parks are places set aside to preserve nature.
    C. Many plants and animals are safe in national parks.

15. What is Banff National Park known for? _____

16. Name two problems facing national parks. _____

17. What is Yellowstone National Park famous for? _____

18. What is a *poacher*?
    A. a fried egg   B. an angry deer   C. an illegal hunter

19. What is the purpose of third paragraph in the selection?
    _____

Algebra/Parts of Speech

DAY 15

Because 2 × 2 = 4, the square root of 4 ($\sqrt{4}$) = 2. Because 2 × 2 × 2 = 8, the cube root of 8 ($\sqrt[3]{8}$) = 2. Identify the square root or cube root.

1. $\sqrt{169}$ = _____
2. $\sqrt{10,000}$ = _____
3. $\sqrt{81}$ = _____

4. $\sqrt[3]{64}$ = _____
5. $\sqrt[3]{512}$ = _____
6. $\sqrt{625}$ = _____

7. $\sqrt[3]{1,728}$ = _____
8. $\sqrt{225}$ = _____
9. $\sqrt{400}$ = _____

10. $\sqrt[3]{216}$ = _____
11. $\sqrt[3]{27,000}$ = _____
12. $\sqrt{2,500}$ = _____

A *coordinating conjunction* connects similar words, phrases, and clauses. Write a coordinating conjunction to complete each sentence.

13. Roses need excellent drainage, _____ their leaves will turn yellow.
14. Eugene wanted a pet that was exotic _____ unusual.
15. It is possible, _____ it is not very likely.
16. We waited in the terminal for hours, _____ our connection never arrived.
17. He was born and raised in Ohio, _____ he now lives in New York.
18. Zoe decides on the itinerary, _____ Joe makes the travel arrangements.
19. Sam has been driving _____ making sales calls for weeks.
20. I cannot attend the wedding, _____ Janet can.
21. Gerald bought celery _____ onions at the grocery store.
22. Carmen _____ Mimi registered for classes.

FACTOID: A newborn giant panda weighs 3–5 ounces (85–142 g).

DAY 15

Literary Terms/Science

Write the letter of the word that matches each definition.

23. _____ a comparison that does not use the words *like* or *as*
24. _____ the formal rhythm of a poem, often used with rhyme
25. _____ a comparison using the word *like* or *as*
26. _____ use of words that start with the same sound
27. _____ a word or phrase that sounds like what it describes
28. _____ use of words that end with the same sound
29. _____ repeated vowel sounds
30. _____ the beat of a poem
31. _____ poetry without a set meter or rhyme scheme

A. alliteration
B. metaphor
C. rhyme
D. assonance
E. meter
F. rhythm
G. free verse
H. onomatopoeia
I. simile

Read the clues that describe each type of rock. Write the correct word from the word bank for each set of clues.

limestone	slate	granite	marble

32. I am an igneous rock.
    I am intrusive.
    I have large mineral grains.
    Because of my strength, I am often used to make headstones.
    Which rock am I? _____

33. I am a sedimentary rock.
    I am made of calcium carbonate.
    I am found where water once stood.
    Gas bubbles appear when acid touches me.
    Which rock am I? _____

34. I am a metamorphic rock.
    I am a foliated rock.
    I am formed from shale.
    My minerals are so compact that I am watertight.
    Which rock am I? _____

35. I am a metamorphic rock.
    I am a non-foliated rock.
    I am formed from limestone.
    Artists often use me to create sculptures.
    Which rock am I? _____

CHARACTER CHECK: At the end of the day, think about how you demonstrated loyalty during the day. Why is loyalty an important quality?

Geometry/Vocabulary

DAY 16

Use the Pythagorean theorem ($a^2 + b^2 = c^2$) to find each missing side length. Round to the nearest hundredth.

1.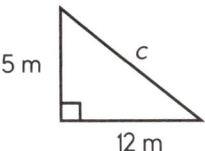
   _____

2.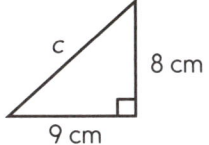
   _____

3.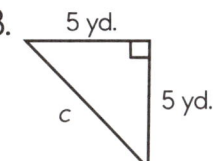
   _____

4.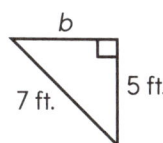
   _____

5.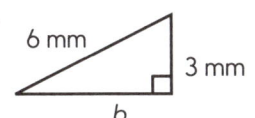
   _____

6.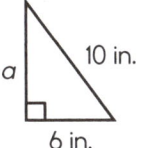
   _____

7.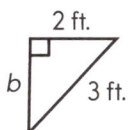
   _____

8.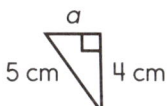
   _____

Circle the letter of the correct meaning for each Greek or Latin root.

9. graph (as in *photograph*)   A. sound   B. written   C. far

10. hydr (as in *hydrant*)   A. water   B. good   C. center

11. aud (as in *audible*)   A. hear   B. see   C. again

12. dict (as in *dictate*)   A. body   B. teach   C. say

13. port (as in *transport*)   A. make   B. carry   C. throw

14. spec (as in *inspector*)   A. see   B. shape   C. send

15. uni (as in *unicycle*)   A. move   B. one   C. many

16. micro (as in *microphone*)   A. much   B. first   C. small

DAY 16

Reading Comprehension/Social Studies

Read the paragraph. Place an *X* by the logical conclusion. Then, underline the facts that helped you reach this conclusion.

Mrs. Jackson saw an advertisement in the newspaper that read, "Final Sale. All watches $35. Available while supplies last. Cash only." Mrs. Jackson needed cash, so she went to the bank. The ATM was broken, so she completed a withdrawal slip and gave it to the teller. "I'm sorry," the teller said as he looked at his computer screen. "You only have $25 in your account."

_____ Mrs. Jackson bought a watch for $25.

_____ The bank teller was mistaken.

_____ Mrs. Jackson was unable to buy a new watch.

_____ Mrs. Jackson bought a unique clock instead.

Write the letter of each ancient empire, civilization, or dynasty next to the phrase that describes it. Some items will be used more than once.

| A. Ancient Greece | B. Incan Empire | C. Mayan Empire |
| D. Roman Empire | E. Tang Dynasty | F. Babylonian Empire |

17. _____ This empire was located in what is now Peru.
18. _____ Its capital was located between the Tigris and Euphrates Rivers.
19. _____ Cuzco, the capital city of this empire, had gardens, paved streets, and stone buildings.
20. _____ The idea of democracy originated with this empire.
21. _____ King Hammurabi created the first set of written laws for this empire.
22. _____ At its peak, it controlled almost all of Europe and parts of Africa.
23. _____ Athens and Sparta were two important city-states of this civilization.
24. _____ It flourished in Central America from about 2600 BC to about AD 900.
25. _____ More than one million people lived in Chang'an, its capital city.
26. _____ This was a period of great cultural achievement in China.

FACTOID: Indonesia has about 13,000 islands, most of which are uninhabited by people.

Geometry/Parts of Speech

DAY 17

Two figures are *congruent* if they are the same size and shape regardless of their orientation. If a figure is rotated (turned), translated (moved), or reflected (flopped) across a line, the two resulting figures are congruent. Decide if the figures are congruent. Write *yes* or *no*.

1.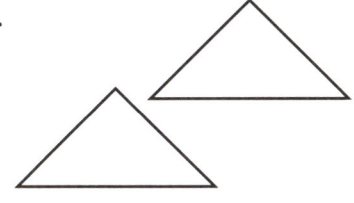

2.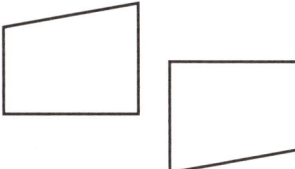

3.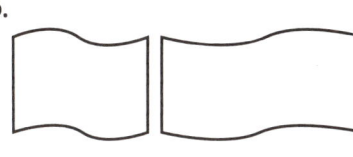

_____   _____   _____

4.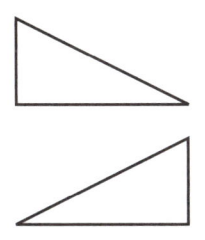

5.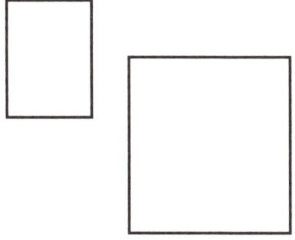

6.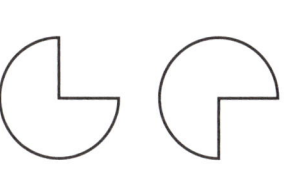

_____   _____   _____

Correlative conjunctions are word pairs that join similar words, phrases, or clauses. The correlative conjunctions are: *both . . . and, neither . . . nor, whether . . . or, either . . . or,* and *not only . . . but* (or *but also*). Write the appropriate correlative conjunctions to complete each sentence.

7. You will need _____ a pencil _____ paper.
8. The toddler drinks _____ milk _____ apple juice.
9. You should ask _____ Rebecca _____ Maria.
10. It is hard to imagine how early scientists worked with _____ scientific equipment _____ any knowledge of experimentation.
11. _____ Jim _____ Brian asked Krystal to dance.
12. I can't decide _____ I want to see a movie _____ eat dinner.
13. The menu includes _____ Italian _____ French food.
14. _____ come with me, _____ I'll go alone.

DAY 17

Reading Comprehension

Read the passage. Then, answer the questions.

Mustangs

The image of horses running freely across the plains is a popular symbol of the American West. However, mustangs are not **indigenous** to the United States. When Spanish armies came to the New World in the sixteenth century, they brought horses with them. Horses had been extinct in the Western hemisphere for about 12,000 years.

The wild horses that now live in the western part of the United States are called *mustangs*. The word comes from the Spanish word *mesteño* meaning *wild* or *stray*. The mustangs' ancestors were Spanish horses that had escaped from Spanish soldiers. American Indian tribes also released horses.

Over many years, the mustang population in western America grew. By the end of the nineteenth century, about two million mustangs roamed the countryside. Farmers and ranchers complained that the mustangs destroyed their crops and ate their livestock's food. Although private conservation efforts began as early as 1925, the mustang population dwindled as many farmers removed the horses from the western plains and prairies. By 1970, fewer than 17,000 mustangs remained in America. In 1971, the U.S. Congress passed a law to protect these wild horses. Today, the government maintains areas that have too many mustangs. Some of the horses are even offered for adoption. About 37,000 mustangs currently live in the United States.

15. Which of the following best defines the word *indigenous*?
    - A. a popular symbol or image
    - B. a breed of wild horse
    - C. native to a particular place
    - D. imported from another country

16. Number the events in the order in which they occurred.
    - _____ About two million mustangs roamed the countryside.
    - _____ Spanish armies brought horses to the New World.
    - _____ Congress passed a law to protect mustangs.
    - _____ Wild horses were extinct in the Western hemisphere.
    - _____ Private conservation efforts began to protect mustangs.

17. Which of the following statements is true?
    - A. The word *mustang* means free and lovely.
    - B. Mustangs have lived in North America since the end of the last Ice Age.
    - C. The first mustangs in the United States had escaped from the Spanish army.

18. Explain the connection between farmers and ranchers and mustangs.

_____

Measurement/Parts of Speech

DAY 18

Find the volume of each solid. Round to the nearest hundredth. Show your work on a separate sheet of paper.

1.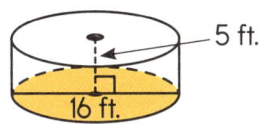

    V = _____

2.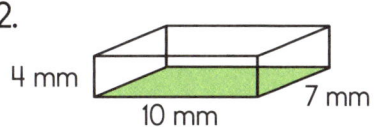

    V = _____

3.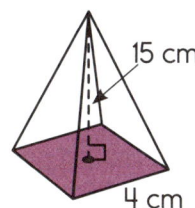

    V = _____

4.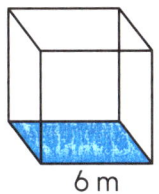

    V = _____

5.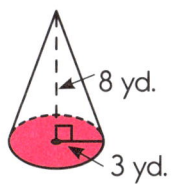

    V = _____

6.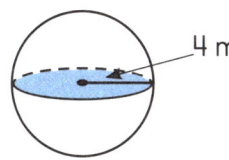

    V = _____

An *interjection* is a word or group of words that expresses emotion. An interjection should be followed by an exclamation point or a comma. Write an interjection to complete each sentence. Then, write two additional sentences that include interjections and appropriate punctuation.

7. _____ I'm not really sure about that.
8. _____ Look at that!
9. _____ Now I understand it better!
10. _____ look! What do you think of this?
11. _____
12. _____

FITNESS FLASH: Do 10 sit-ups.

* See page ii.

DAY 18

Literary Terms/Science

A story's setting tells the time and place of the action. Read each phrase. Write *T* if a phrase indicates time. Write *P* if a phrase indicates place. Then, add a time and a place of your own to the list.

13. _____ after midnight
14. _____ on Tuesday
15. _____ before sundown
16. _____ by the gate
17. _____ in the dead of winter
18. _____ 45 minutes later
19. _____ after the typhoon
20. _____ at twilight
21. _____ in the large cafeteria
22. _____ in the tropics
23. _____ before dawn
24. _____ near the berry patch
25. _____ near the sculpture
26. _____ at the entrance to the theater
27. _____
28. _____

Write the correct word from the word bank for each definition.

| acceleration | friction | inertia | momentum | speed |
| force | gravity | | mass | weight | velocity |

29. _____ the force that pulls objects toward each other
30. _____ the distance that an object travels in a given time
31. _____ the speed in a given direction
32. _____ the force of gravity on an object at a planet's surface
33. _____ the force one object exerts on another when they rub together
34. _____ the pushing or pulling on an object
35. _____ the product of an object's mass times its velocity
36. _____ the tendency of an object to resist any change in its motion
37. _____ the rate at which an object's velocity changes
38. _____ the amount of matter in an object

FACTOID: The ice at the south pole is about 9,000 feet (2,743 m) thick.

Geometry/Data Analysis

DAY 19

Classify each triangle by examining its angles and sides.

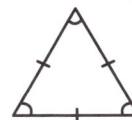 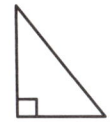 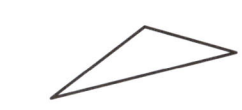

1. _____   2. _____   3. _____

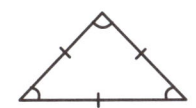  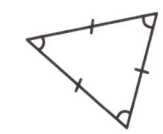

4. _____   5. _____   6. _____

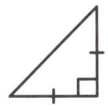  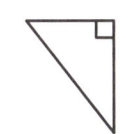

7. _____   8. _____   9. _____

Use the data set below to plot ordered pairs (x, y) and create a scatter plot. Draw a line of best fit, or a straight line that shows the general direction of the points. Then, answer the questions.

Weight (lb.)	Mileage (mi./gal.)
2750	29
3125	23
2100	33
4082	18
3640	21
2241	25

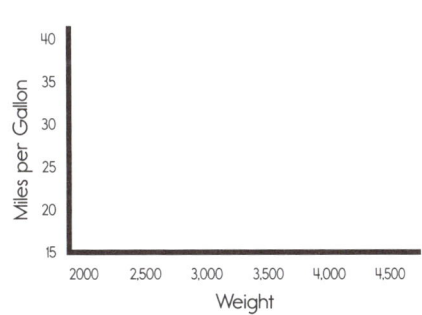

10. What two data sets are being compared by this scatter plot? _____
_____

11. Is the correlation between weight and miles per gallon positive (values that increase together) or negative (one value increases while the other decreases)?
_____

    How do you know? _____

DAY 19

Circle the letter next to the best reference for researching each topic.

12. In which reference would you look for general information about the Mayan culture?
    A. dictionary
    B. atlas
    C. almanac
    D. encyclopedia

13. In which reference would you find a chart for plants in different world regions?
    A. atlas
    B. encyclopedia
    C. newspaper
    D. almanac

14. In which reference would you find publication information about a short story?
    A. book of quotations
    B. encyclopedia
    C. literary magazine
    D. newspaper

15. In which reference would you find a word or phrase that means the same as *somber*?
    A. telephone directory
    B. newspaper
    C. encyclopedia
    D. thesaurus

16. In which reference would you find a famous saying from Thomas Edison?
    A. atlas
    B. encyclopedia
    C. book of quotations
    D. almanac

17. In which reference would you find the origin of the word *umbrella*?
    A. dictionary
    B. newspaper
    C. almanac
    D. book of quotations

Think of different fortunes you might read in a fortune cookie. If you could make one fortune come true, what would it be and why?

_____

_____

_____

FITNESS FLASH: Do 10 squats.

* See page ii.

Algebra/Parts of Speech

DAY 20

Find the value of the variable in each equation.

1. $5x - 24 = 101$
2. $\frac{y}{12} - 7 = 13$
3. $12 + 8w = 76$
4. $50 - 3a = 122$
5. $\frac{r}{49} = 7$
6. $62 + 12m = -10$
7. $7b - 80 = 4$
8. $x^2 - 24 = 300$
9. $45 - 3k = 117$
10. $8c + 100 = -12$
11. $\frac{x}{9} - 32 = 9$
12. $\frac{y}{3} - 15 = 45$

A *gerund* is a verb that is used as a noun. To form a gerund, add *-ing* to the base verb. Circle the gerund in each sentence. Then, write its base verb on the line.

13. _____ A very important step is knowing what to do.
14. _____ I love hearing our band play John Philip Sousa's marches.
15. _____ When I swim, my favorite activity is floating on my back.
16. _____ Complaining never works with my parents.
17. _____ More than any other part of golf, I like putting the best.
18. _____ Going to the library with her dad was one of Shari's favorite things to do when she was a child.

An *infinitive* is formed by *to* + a simple verb. In a sentence, it can be used as a noun, adjective, or adverb. Underline the infinitive in each sentence.

19. To snowboard in the Rocky Mountains is a dream of mine.
20. On Saturday mornings, there are always chores to do.
21. Lately, the favorite pastime among my friends is to play laser tag.
22. Maya raced down the field to attempt another shot on goal.
23. Achiro wanted a good grade on the test, so he stayed up late to study.

FACTOID: More than one-fifth of the land on Earth is desert.

Read the passage. Then, answer the questions.

Chambered Nautilus

The chambered nautilus is a modern, living fossil. It belongs to a group of mollusks called *cephalopods* and is related to the octopus, squid, and cuttlefish. Unlike its cousins, the nautilus has an external shell consisting of many chambers. The animal lives in the outermost chamber and uses the rest to regulate its buoyancy, or ability to sink and float. The chambered nautilus lives in the Indian and South Pacific Oceans, finding its home at depths of 900 to 2,000 feet (274 m to 610 m) along reef walls. On dark, moonless nights, it travels closer to the surface to eat tiny fish, shrimp, and the molted shells of spiny lobsters. The chambered nautilus cannot change color or squirt ink like its relatives, but it does have arms. Two rows of 80 to 100 tentacles surround its head. None have suckers to hold prey, but each can touch and taste. The nautilus lives longer than other cephalopods—sometimes up to 20 years. Unlike the octopus, it mates many times during its lifetime, each time attaching its eggs to rocks, coral, or the seafloor. Each egg takes about one year to hatch. Humans are the main threat to this ancient creature's continued survival.

24. Where does the chambered nautilus live? _____

25. Describe the chambered nautilus. _____
_____

26. What does the chambered nautilus eat? _____

27. What happens to the nautilus's eggs?
_____

28. In the passage, underline a similarity between the chambered nautilus and the other cephalopods.

29. In the passage, circle a difference between the chambered nautilus and the other cephalopods.

CHARACTER CHECK: Keep a tally throughout the day of the number of times you show respect toward others. Share the results with a family member.

Science Experiment

BONUS

Convection Currents

Boiling water creates currents that rise and sink because of uneven heat. Hot, less dense water rises. As the hot water reaches the surface, it cools and sinks to the bottom of the pot again. This process mimics what molten rocks do within Earth's mantle. These rising and falling movements are called *convection currents*.

Materials:
- 9" x 13" x 2" (32 cm x 23 cm x 5 cm) clear, glass baking dish that is safe for stovetop cooking
- stovetop
- food coloring
- water
- oven mitts

Procedure:
Fill the baking dish halfway with water. Carefully place the dish on the stovetop. With adult supervision, turn the stove on low. The dish will become hot. Remove the dish from the stovetop. Caution: Wear oven mitts to handle the baking dish. Add a few drops of food coloring to the water in the center of the dish. Observe the movement of the water in the dish. In the chart below, draw a diagram of what happens. Add food coloring to different locations in the dish. Again, draw a diagram of what happens.

Left Side	Center	Right Side

1. Describe the convection currents that occurred as the water heated.

   _____

   _____

2. In your own words, describe what caused the convection currents that occurred in the dish.

   _____

   _____

* See page ii.

© Carson Dellosa Education

BONUS

Science Experiment

Engineering for Earthquakes

Engineers who design buildings for earthquake-prone areas must keep the possibility of earthquakes in mind. People can be injured by the total or partial collapse of a building or by glass falling from structures. It would be difficult to create an earthquake-proof building. Instead, engineers create earthquake-resistant buildings that may suffer damage during an earthquake but keep people inside and within the immediate vicinity safe. In this activity, you will build a model of an earthquake-resistant skyscraper.

Materials:
- 8 to 10 building blocks
- dictionary
- craft sticks
- rubber bands
- toothpicks
- yardstick or meterstick

Procedure:
On a table, stack 8 to 10 blocks to create a skyscraper. Draw a picture of the skyscraper in the chart. Hold a dictionary about one yard (one meter) above the table. Drop it onto the table next to the skyscraper to create an "earthquake." Record your observations. Use the blocks and the other building materials to try to create a skyscraper that will resist the shaking caused by the "earthquake." Draw a picture of the new skyscraper in the chart. Then, drop the dictionary on the table again. Record your observations. Include why the first skyscraper toppled and how you altered the second skyscraper to make it earthquake resistant.

Drawing of First Skyscraper	Drawing of New Skyscraper

Effect of First Earthquake	Effect of Second Earthquake

Social Studies Activity

BONUS

Latitude and Longitude: United States and Canada

Lines of latitude and longitude form an imaginary grid over the Earth to help determine any absolute location. An absolute location is the definitive location of a place using a recognized coordinate system. Relative location is a place's location in relation to other nearby places.

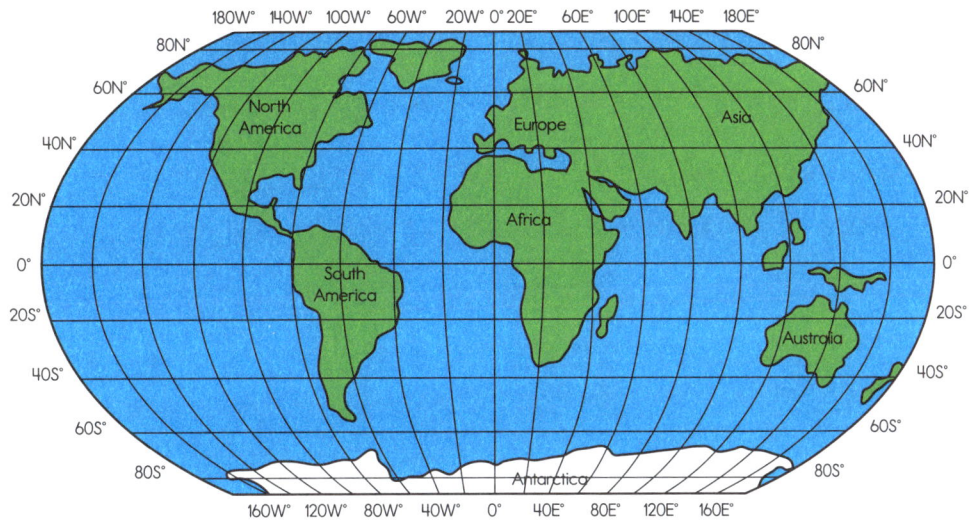

Use an atlas to answer the following questions about locations in the United States and Canada.

1. Which state includes the intersection of 35°N and 120°W? _____
2. Which province is located north of Idaho, east of British Columbia, and west of Saskatchewan? _____
3. Which ocean includes the intersection of 30°N and 30°W? _____
4. Which state is located north of Florida, east of Alabama, west of the Atlantic Ocean, and southwest of South Carolina? _____
5. Which state includes the intersection of 35°N and 105°W? _____
6. Which ocean includes the intersection of 75°N and 135°W? _____
7. Which mountains cross the 120°W line of longitude? _____
8. Which line of latitude is the border between Nebraska and Kansas? _____
9. Which line of latitude follows the northern border of four provinces? _____
10. Which lines of latitude and longitude intersect in Illinois? _____
11. What line of longitude does the Mississippi River cross? _____

© Carson Dellosa Education

Social Studies Activity

BONUS

The Role of Government

A government can provide services for many of its citizens' needs. Its primary functions involve making, implementing, and enforcing laws and managing any conflicts about laws. A government also provides for the nation's defense.

Match each need on the right with the corresponding government service on the left. More than one government service may meet the same need.

1. _____ education
2. _____ communication
3. _____ safety
4. _____ national defense
5. _____ transportation
6. _____ health
7. _____ help for the needy
8. _____ clean air and water
9. _____ money to trade for goods

A. print money
B. provide a police force
C. build roads
D. provide unemployment benefits
E. fund and staff public schools
F. inspect food and medications
G. deliver mail
H. make laws to restrict pollution
I. fund, staff, and train armed forces

International Services

Research the services that are provided by the United Nations, the World Health Organization, UNICEF, or other international aid organizations. Write a paragraph comparing the services that are offered to the services listed in the activity above.

_____
_____
_____
_____
_____
_____
_____
_____
_____

Social Studies Activity

BONUS

If Landmarks Could Talk

Some buildings, landmarks, and natural features are so well-known that you may recognize them even if you have never seen them in person. Identify the following places by reading the clues. Then, use reference materials to check your answers.

1. I am a famous attraction in the United States. I am 279 miles (449 km) long and 1 mile (1.6 km) deep. People come from all over the world to hike in and around me.

    _____

2. Built by an emperor as a tomb for his wife, I am one of the most beautiful buildings in the world. I am found about 105 miles (169 km) southeast of New Delhi, India.

    _____

3. I have stood for almost 2,500 years on a hill called the Acropolis. The people of Greece built me to honor the goddess Athena.

    _____

4. Famous for my giant, stone statues of huge heads with long ears, I am found about 2,300 miles (3,700 km) west of Chile in the Pacific Ocean.

    _____

5. Built completely by hand, I am the longest structure ever built. I stretch about 4,000 miles (6,400 km) across northern China.

    _____

6. Located in the largest city in Australia, about 425 miles (684 km) northeast of Melbourne, I stand on the waterfront and look like a giant sailboat.

    _____

7. I was built to house cathedral bells. But, the soil on which I stand is too soft, so I do not stand completely upright. I am found in a city about 42 miles (68 km) west and just south of Florence, Italy.

    _____

8. I am an ancient monument that may have been used as a ceremonial or religious center. I am made of a group of huge stones arranged in a circle on a plain in southwestern England.

    _____

9. I am an enormous limestone statue with the head of a human and the body of a lion. Built about 4,500 years ago in Egypt, I stand 66 feet (20 m) tall, and I am 240 feet (73 m) long.

    _____

10. Erected as a memorial to honor four U.S. presidents, I am carved into a South Dakota mountain.

    _____

DAY 20

Outdoor Extension Activities

Take It Outside!

With an adult, take a pen and a notebook outside during the early morning. Write what you see and hear. Reflect on your morning observations. Just before dusk, go outside again with an adult to the same spot. Record the sights and sounds you hear at this time of the day. Then, compare your notes of day and night activity. How do the morning observations compare with what you saw and heard at dusk? Write a poem or essay comparing the two times of day. Create an illustration that captures the mood to accompany the poem or essay.

With family members, visit a local adventure park for a day. Bring a camera and take pictures of various adventure rides. Then, print the pictures and create a collage of the rides. Label each photo to indicate which rides produce thrills with motion or by force. Share your collage and findings with your family and explain how the rides use force and motion.

With a family member, visit different areas in your community. Bring a camera. Look for triangle shapes that have been used in the design or construction of buildings. When you spot a triangle, take a picture. Print the pictures and look for similarities and differences in how the triangles are used. Make a photo album, noting how simple triangle shapes can add character to your community. Tally the number of examples that you found for each type of triangle: equilateral, isosceles, scalene, and right. Which was the hardest to find? Which was the easiest?

Triangle Type	Number of Examples
equilateral	
isosceles	
scalene	
right	

* See page ii.

SECTION III

Monthly Goals

Think of three goals to set for yourself this month. For example, you may want to learn five new vocabulary words each week. Write your goals on the lines. Post them somewhere that you will see them every day.

Draw a check mark beside each goal you meet. Feel proud that you have met your goals and continue to set new ones to challenge yourself.

1. _____
2. _____
3. _____

Word List

The following words are used in this section. Use a dictionary to look up each word that you do not know. Then, write three sentences. Use at least one word from the word list in each sentence.

    dynasty   phases
    immortalized   quenched
    maxim   unison
    omitted   verge
    output   wrench

1. _____
_____
2. _____
_____
3. _____
_____

SECTION III

Introduction to Endurance

This section includes fitness and character development activities that focus on endurance. These activities are designed to get you moving and thinking about developing your physical and mental stamina.

Physical Endurance

What do climbing stairs, jogging, and riding your bike have in common? They are all great ways to build endurance!

Having endurance means performing an activity for a period of time before your body becomes tired. Improving your endurance requires regular aerobic exercise, which causes your heart to beat faster. You also breathe harder. As a result of regular aerobic activity, your heart becomes stronger, and your blood cells deliver oxygen to your body more efficiently.

Summer provides numerous opportunities to improve your endurance. Although there are times when a relaxing activity is valuable, it is important to take advantage of the warm mornings and sunny days to go outside. Choose activities that you enjoy. Invite a family member to go for a walk or a bike ride. Play a game of basketball with friends. Leave the relaxing activities for when it is dark, too hot, or raining.

Set an endurance goal this summer. For example, you might jog every day until you can run one mile without stopping. Set new goals when you meet your old ones. Be proud of your endurance success!

Mental Endurance

Endurance applies to the mind as well as to the body. Showing mental endurance means persevering. You can show mental endurance every day. Continuing with tasks when you might want to quit and working until they are done are ways that you can show mental endurance.

Build your mental endurance this summer. Maybe you want to earn some extra money for a new bike by helping your neighbors with yard work. But, after one week of working in your neighbors' yards, it is not as easy as you thought it would be. Think about some key points, such as how you have wanted that new bike for months. Be positive. Remind yourself that you have been working for only one week and that your neighbors are very appreciative of your work. Think of ways to make the yard work more enjoyable, such as starting earlier in the day or listening to music while you work. Quitting should be the last resort.

Build your mental endurance now. It will help prepare you for challenges later.

Geometry/Language Arts

DAY 1

Find each missing angle measurement or side length.

1.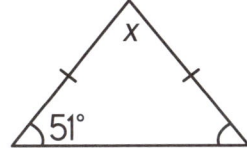
_____

2.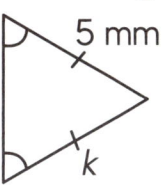
_____

3.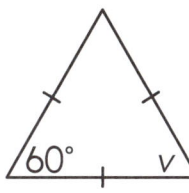
_____

4.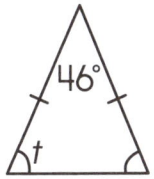
_____

5.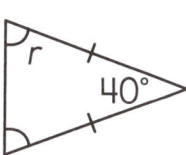
_____

6.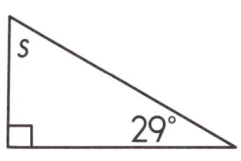
_____

An *ellipsis*, or three dots spaced closely together (…), shows that something has been omitted. When quoting a text, writers often choose to omit words in order to make sentences shorter or to focus on important points. Rewrite sentences from *The Gettysburg Address*. Replace underlined words with ellipses.

7. Four score and seven years ago our fathers brought forth <u>on this continent,</u> a new nation<u>, conceived in Liberty, and</u> dedicated to the proposition that all men are created equal.

_____
_____
_____

8. Now we are engaged in a great civil war, testing whether that nation<u>, or any nation so conceived and so dedicated,</u> can long endure.

_____
_____
_____

9. But, in a larger sense, we cannot dedicate—<u>we cannot consecrate—we cannot hallow —</u>this ground.

_____
_____
_____

DAY 1

Vocabulary/Multiplication & Division

Read each word. Write the root word, the prefix, and the suffix in the correct columns. Some words will have either a prefix or a suffix, and some words may have both a prefix and a suffix.

	Prefix	Root Word	Suffix
10. expressible			
11. unbelievable			
12. dramatize			
13. allowance			
14. researcher			

The chart gives sample currency exchange rates between U.S. dollars and several other currencies.

Currencies	What the Currency Equals in U.S. Dollars	What US$1 Equals in the Currency
Canadian dollar	$1.03	0.974 Canadian dollars
Russian ruble	$0.04	27.84 rubles
Japanese yen	$0.0127	78.95 yen
Indian rupee	$0.0224	44.56 rupees

15. Complete the chart to find the cost of a soft drink in U.S. dollars in each country. The first one has been done for you.

Your $5	×	What US$1 Equals in the Currency	=	What US$5 Equals in the Currency	−	Cost of a Soft Drink in the Currency	=	Your Change in the Currency	×	What the Currency Equals in U.S. Dollars	=	Your Change in U.S. Dollars	Cost of a Soft Drink in U.S. Dollars
A. US$5	×	0.974 dollars (Canadian)	=	4.87 dollars (Canadian)	−	1.35 dollars (Canadian)	=	3.52 dollars (Canadian)	×	$1.03	=	$3.63	$1.37
B. US$5	×	27.84 rubles	=	____ rubles	−	35 rubles	=	____ rubles	×	$0.04	=	$4.17	$____
C. US$5	×	78.95 yen	=	394.75 yen	−	120 yen	=	____ yen	×	$0.0127	=	$3.49	$____
D. US$5	×	44.56 rupees	=	222.80 rupees	−	150 rupees	=	72.80 rupees	×	$0.0224	=	$____	$____

FACTOID: The Peregrine falcon can dive at a speed of 200 miles per hour.

Geometry/Algebra

DAY 2

Make a drawing based on the information in the problem. Then, use the Pythagorean theorem ($a^2 + b^2 = c^2$) to solve. Round answers to the nearest tenth.

1. A 16-foot ladder leans against the side of a building. The top of the ladder touches the side of the building at 12 feet above the ground. How far away from the base of the building is the bottom of the ladder?

   The ladder stands _____ feet from the building.

2. A tree casts a 24 m shadow along the ground, measured from the tree's trunk to the farthest edge of the shadow. The measurement from the top of the tree to the farthest edge of the shadow is 80 m. How tall is the tree?

   The tree is _____ m tall.

Approximate the value of each expression.

3. The value of $\sqrt{10}$ is between _____ and _____.
4. The value of $\sqrt[3]{74}$ is between _____ and _____.
5. The value of $\sqrt{43}$ is between _____ and _____.
6. The value of $\sqrt[3]{17}$ is between _____ and _____.
7. The value of $\sqrt[3]{2}$ is between _____ and _____.
8. The value of $\sqrt{24}$ is between _____ and _____.

Put the values in order from least to greatest along the number line.

9. 14, $\sqrt{18}$, 4π

10. $\sqrt{5}$, 2, 5

DAY 2

Vocabulary/Writing

Circle the answer that correctly completes each analogy.

11. poet: verses :: _____
    A. cooper: shoes
    B. cobbler: hats
    C. novelist: music
    D. cartographer: maps

12. virtuoso: mediocre :: _____
    A. novice: inexperienced
    B. talented: gifted
    C. recluse: sociable
    D. nomad: itinerant

13. valiant: courage :: _____
    A. chipper: melancholy
    B. wrathful: boredom
    C. tyrannical: power
    D. frightened: effrontery

14. dexterity: nimble :: _____
    A. integrity: duplicitous
    B. complacent: eager
    C. novel: pamphlet
    D. hubris: arrogance

15. gale: wind :: _____
    A. deluge: rain
    B. snow: blizzard
    C. flood: tidal wave
    D. frostbite: cold

16. apple: tree :: _____
    A. fruit: vegetable
    B. grape: vine
    C. plum: pear
    D. banana: peel

You have just been hired as a reporter for the *Way Out There* world newspaper, specializing in unique and wacky news. Create a headline for your first news story. Then, write the news story to accompany your headline. You may quote imaginary scientists, authorities, or other sources. Use another piece of paper if you need more space.

_____
_____
_____
_____
_____
_____

FITNESS FLASH: Jog in place for 30 seconds.

* See page ii.

Multiplication/Parts of Speech

DAY 3

Write each number in scientific notation.

EXAMPLES: $800{,}000 = \mathbf{8 \times 10^5}$ $0.00285 = \mathbf{2.85 \times 10^{-3}}$

1. $250{,}000 =$ _____
2. $0.00012 =$ _____
3. $3{,}650{,}000 =$ _____
4. $45{,}000{,}000{,}000 =$ _____
5. $0.000096 =$ _____
6. $123{,}000 =$ _____

Write each number in standard form.

7. $3.2 \times 10^5 =$ _____
8. $6.41 \times 10^{-7} =$ _____
9. $1.2 \times 10^9 =$ _____
10. $7.04 \times 10^3 =$ _____
11. $1.14 \times 10^{-6} =$ _____
12. $1.09 \times 10^7 =$ _____

A verb in the *indicative* mood expresses a fact or an opinion.
EXAMPLE: I like to rollerblade.

A verb in the *imperative* mood expresses a command or a request.
EXAMPLE: Bake the bread for 45 minutes.

A verb in the *interrogative* mood asks a question.
EXAMPLE: Did Shyla return the books yet?

A verb in the *conditional* mood expresses something that is dependent on a condition.
EXAMPLE: If I had enough money, I would have bought a new MP3 player.

Read each sentence. Identify the verb mood by writing *I* (indicative), *IM* (imperative), *IN* (interrogative), or *C* (conditional) on the line.

13. _____ The owl flew across the yard on almost-silent wings.
14. _____ Has Eduardo started taking rock climbing lessons?
15. _____ Ask Thomas if he's ready to leave.
16. _____ If my sister were older, she could go on the field trip.
17. _____ Will you help me carry these boxes?
18. _____ Bring the entire stack of books with you.
19. _____ Georgia wore a cast for six weeks.
20. _____ If we could spend the night at Ian's house, we would promise to go to bed early.
21. _____ Luna turned the fan on high.
22. _____ Can a panther run faster than a jaguar?

DAY 3

Reading Comprehension

Read the passage. Then, answer the questions.

Taking a Poll

A poll is a survey of random opinions to be analyzed for a specific purpose. A classroom poll might ask students to name their favorite foods or their favorite musical groups. The polling question should always be neutral so that the results are not biased. This means that the question must not influence the answer. For example, the question *I do not like pizza, do you?* may bias the respondent to agree with the question instead of provide a true opinion. Large groups can be polled by using a **subsample**, or smaller representative group, instead of polling every person. The subsample should be chosen at random. To find out which sport eighth-graders at your local middle school like best, you might make a list of their names and ask every third person for an opinion. However, if you polled only eighth-graders at the park, your sample might be biased toward people who already play sports there.

23. What is the main idea of this passage?
    A. People who like sports often go to the park.
    B. You can take a poll to learn about people's favorite foods.
    C. A poll should be unbiased and include a random sample.

24. What does it mean to conduct an unbiased poll?
    A. to visit the park and ask people their favorite sport
    B. to ask a question in a way that does not influence the people who are answering
    C. to talk to only eighth graders about their favorite sports

25. What is an unbiased way of asking the polling question about sports in the passage? _____
    _____

26. What is a *subsample*? _____
    _____

27. How can a large group of people be polled without talking to every person?
    _____

FACTOID: The average summer temperature in Antarctica is 35.6°F (2°C).

Algebra/Language Arts

DAY 4

You can use the *slope-intercept form* to graph linear equations. In the example below, 5 is the y-intercept, or the point (0, 5) at which the line crosses the y-axis. $\frac{2}{1}$, or the absolute value of the coefficient of x expressed as a fraction, is the slope. To graph the line, start at the y-intercept and plot points by counting 2 up and 1 right on the coordinate plane.

Use the slope-intercept form to graph each system of equations. Then, give the coordinates of the point (x, y) where the lines intersect to solve the system.

EXAMPLE: $y = 2x + 5$ ← y-intercept (0, 5)

Slope, or rate of change; change to fraction $\frac{2}{1}$.

1. $y = x + 4$
   $y = 2x$

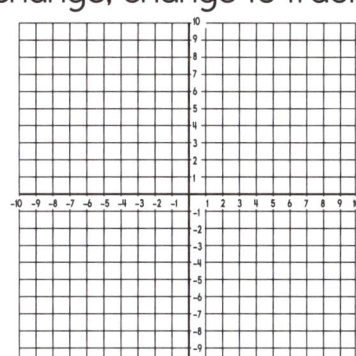

Coordinates of point of intersection: _____

2. $y = 2x - 2$
   $y = -x + 7$

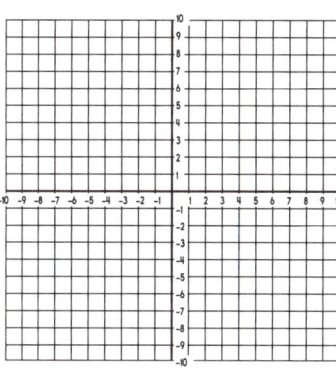

Coordinates of point of intersection: _____

Dashes that surround words in a sentence can be used to indicate a sudden break or a change in thought. Rewrite each sentence, adding dashes where needed.

EXAMPLE: After the game—I hope the Cardinals win—we're going to have a cookout.

3. My aunt she lives just a few miles away has a horse and six chickens.

   _____

4. Enrique texted his best friend he just got a new phone to see what Colin's plans were for the weekend.

   _____
   _____

5. After you've mixed in the mashed bananas make sure you've sprayed the pan with cooking spray you can carefully scrape the batter into the pan.

   _____
   _____

DAY 4

Vocabulary/Fitness

Read each sentence. Use context clues to match each boldfaced word with its definition.

6. _____ My uncle used a hammer to **wrench** the nail from the board.
7. _____ Daniel auditioned for a **role** in the school play.
8. _____ Silk has a very smooth **texture**.
9. _____ Our class answered the question in **unison**.
10. _____ The teacher accidentally **omitted** Cathy's name from the list.
11. _____ We learned about the **phases** of the moon in science class.
12. _____ Tony **quenched** his thirst after the race by drinking water.
13. _____ Scientists believed that they were on the **verge** of finding a cure for the disease.
14. _____ "Actions speak louder than words" is an old **maxim**.

A. a part played by an actor
B. at the edge
C. general rule or truth
D. left out
E. stages
F. satisfied
G. at the same time
H. pull out
I. characteristics of a surface

Make Endurance Routine!

Endurance is the ability to perform a physical activity for an extended period of time. There are many ways to build endurance. For this activity, you will need a jump rope and a stopwatch.

To begin, walk briskly in place for two minutes to warm up. Then, jog in place for one minute. Jump rope for two minutes and do jumping jacks for one minute. To cool down and complete your routine, walk in place for one minute. Catch your breath. Repeat this activity if possible, or set an endurance goal for completing this activity.

To make this activity more challenging, gradually increase the length of each exercise and change the order of the activities.

FITNESS FLASH: Do 10 jumping jacks.

* See page ii.

Algebra/Parts of Speech

DAY 5

Write an equation to describe each function table.

EXAMPLE:

input (x)	output (y)
1	5
2	8
3	11

Equation: $y = 3x + 2$

1.

input (x)	output (y)
3	−5
6	−4
9	−3

Equation: _____

2.

input (x)	output (y)
2	9
5	15
7	19

Equation: _____

3.

input (x)	output (y)
4	10
8	16
10	19

Equation: _____

4.

input (x)	output (y)
2	11
4	23
5	30

Equation: _____

5.

input (x)	output (y)
2	−7
4	−11
6	−15

Equation: _____

Write a sentence to illustrate each verb mood.

6. Indicative: _____

7. Imperative: _____

8. Interrogative: _____

9. Conditional: _____

DAY 5

Language Arts/Science

Jargon is an expression directed at a specialized audience, such as sports fans. *Slang* is informal language that may be inappropriate for some occasions or may become quickly outdated. Avoid jargon and slang when writing for a general audience.

Read each sentence. Circle the jargon or slang. Write words that better express the jargon or slang.

10. Jake said that the group's new song was very cool. _____
11. "I read it twice," said Mark. "But, I still don't get it." _____
12. Bert gave me props for my high score on the test. _____
13. "What's up?" asked Dr. Marvel as he greeted his students. _____
14. The dress Suzie wore is really in right now. _____
15. The Morton family wanted to chill, so they stayed home all weekend and rested.
    _____
16. Tammy studied for the physics exam for so long that she knew she would hit it out of the park.
    _____

Write the letter of the word from the word bank that matches each definition.

| A. producer | B. consumer | C. decomposer | D. carnivore |
| E. scavenger | F. herbivore | G. omnivore | |

17. _____ an organism that breaks down dead organisms and waste
18. _____ an organism that cannot create its own food, so it eats other organisms
19. _____ an organism that eats the remains of dead animals
20. _____ an organism that eats only plants
21. _____ an organism that eats both plants and animals
22. _____ an organism that creates its own food through photosynthesis
23. _____ an organism that eats only animals

CHARACTER CHECK: What does *perseverance* mean? Write about a time when you showed perseverance.

Geometry/Grammar

DAY 6

Use the figure to answer the questions.

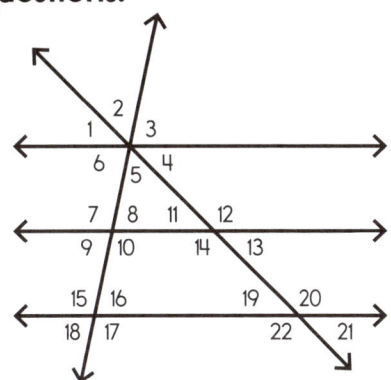

1. If the measure of ∠1 is 45°, what is the measure of ∠13? _____
2. If the measure of ∠11 is 45°, what is the measure of ∠12? _____
3. If the measure of ∠8 is 85°, what is the measure of ∠5? _____
4. If the measure of ∠20 is 135°, what is the measure of ∠21? _____
5. Is the triangle formed by ∠5, ∠8, and ∠11 similar to the triangle formed by ∠5, ∠16, and ∠19? _____

   How do you know? _____

Read each group of words. Write *C* if the group of words is a complete sentence. Write *F* if the group of words is a sentence fragment.

6. _____ Kelly and the red balloon
7. _____ Although a former soldier and a member of Congress
8. _____ After finding the answer to her question, Coleen printed the story as proof
9. _____ Fell coming out of the starting block but made up lots of ground
10. _____ Unless you buy a ticket
11. _____ Many of my friends love to play video games
12. _____ Who would have had a clue that he would win

Write a complete sentence using this sentence fragment.

13. Until the end of the semester _____

_____

DAY 6

Reading Comprehension

Read the passage. Then, answer the questions.

The Ides of March

William Shakespeare **immortalized** the phrase *the ides of March*. In Shakespeare's play *Julius Caesar*, Caesar asks a soothsayer, or fortune teller, what his future holds. Caesar is told, "Beware the ides of March!" It is a phrase that is still used today.

The ides of March means the *15th of March*. The Roman calendar built its months around three types of days: calends (the 1st day of the month), nones (the 7th day of the month), and ides (either the 13th or 15th day of the month). In some months, the ides fell on the 15th day of the month. In other months, the ides fell on the 13th day. Romans identified the other days of the month by counting backward or forward from the calends, nones, or ides. For example, the 18th day of a month would be three days after the ides. Every month had an ides, but the ides of March has historical significance because Julius Caesar was assassinated in 44 BC on the 15th of March.

Aside from the ides of March, the Romans provided the basis for our modern-day calendar system of 365.25 days per year and 366 days during a leap year. The Romans also gave us the word *calendar*, which originates from their word *calends*. So, we have Shakespeare and the Ancient Romans to thank for the term *ides of March*.

14. Which best summarizes the main idea of this passage?
    A. The Roman calendar only had three days.
    B. Julius Caesar was assassinated on the ides of March.
    C. The *ides of March* is a popular term because of Shakespeare's *Julius Caesar*.

15. Which of the following best defines the word *immortalized*?
    A. explained clearly
    B. accented
    C. made to last forever
    D. to tell the future

16. In Shakespeare's play, why did the soothsayer tell Caesar, "Beware the ides of March"?
    A. He was predicting Caesar's assassination.
    B. He had met Caesar, and he did not like him.
    C. He was addressing a very important man.

17. Do any other common expressions originate from Shakespeare's plays? Which of these expressions are still in use today? Do some research to answer this question and write your response on a separate sheet of paper.

FACTOID: Two stars that orbit each other are called *doubles*. About half of the stars in the universe are doubles.

Algebra/Vocabulary

DAY 7

In a *function*, each input value (*x*) corresponds to one output value (*y*). Complete each function table.

1. $y = 2x + 7$

x	y
-7	___
-4	___
0	___
2	___
5	___

2. $y = -8x - 4$

x	y
-10	___
-3	___
1	___
2	___
3	___

3. $y = \frac{x}{2} + 4$

x	y
-4	___
-2	___
0	___
8	___
11	___

4. $y = 3x - 11$

x	y
-6	___
-1	___
1	___
3	___
5	___

5. $y = -\frac{-x}{4} + 4$

x	y
-16	___
-4	___
0	___
5	___
9	___

6. $y = x - 15$

x	y
-40	___
-23	___
-16	___
12	___
30	___

The words in each set have similar denotations but different connotations. Write a sentence for each word in which the context fits the connotation.

7. cheap: _____

   thrifty: _____

   miserly: _____

8. childlike: _____

   immature: _____

   youthful: _____

9. slim: _____

   scrawny: _____

   lean: _____

DAY 7

Reading Comprehension/Social Studies

Read the passage. What conclusion can you draw about Jon's future education? Write your conclusion. Use a separate piece of paper if you need more space.

Jon was worried. He anticipated that the envelope would arrive in the mail that day. If the envelope was large, it meant that he was accepted to the college of his choice. He reasoned that a large envelope meant that there were many forms to complete as part of the registration process. On the other hand, a small envelope might mean bad news. A small envelope meant that it held only one piece of paper—a letter indicating that he was not accepted.

Just then, the doorbell rang. "Delivery," announced Mr. Foxman, the mail carrier. Jon raced to the door. "Gee," said Mr. Foxman, handing Jon the envelope, "they needed extra postage for this one."

_____

_____

Write the letter of each U.S. document next to its description.

10. _____ defined the rights of U.S. citizens in relation to the Constitution

11. _____ allowed the United States to purchase the land west of the Mississippi River from France

12. _____ four-page document, which was signed in 1787, established the U.S. government

13. _____ closed colonization of the Western Hemisphere

14. _____ served as the first U.S. Constitution

15. _____ issued by President Lincoln during the Civil War, it freed all slaves in the Confederate states

16. _____ provided a method for admitting new states into the country

17. _____ stated that the 13 original colonies were no longer subject to British rule

A. Declaration of Independence
B. Articles of Confederation
C. Northwest Ordinance
D. Monroe Doctrine
E. Bill of Rights
F. Louisiana Purchase Treaty
G. U.S. Constitution
H. Emancipation Proclamation

FITNESS FLASH: Hop on your left foot 10 times.

* See page ii.

Algebra/Vocabulary

DAY 8

A function is *linear* if its values have a constant rate of change, or slope. If the slope is not constant, the function is *nonlinear*. To decide, use the formula $\frac{y_2 - y_1}{x_2 - x_1}$ across multiple points. Write *linear* or *nonlinear* beside each function table.

EXAMPLE:

x	y	Rate
1	217	217
2	434	
3	651	217
4	868	

Relationship: __linear__

1.

x	y	Rate
−1	0	
0	−5	
1	−8	
2	−9	

Relationship: _____

2.

x	y	Rate
−3	−15	
1	−8	
5	−1	
9	6	

Relationship: _____

3.

x	y	Rate
0	2	
1	4	
2	10	
3	28	

Relationship: _____

4.

x	y	Rate
10	327	
20	342	
30	357	
40	372	

Relationship: _____

Use a print or online thesaurus to find a synonym for each boldface word. Write the synonym on the line.

5. I tend to be strong-willed and **obstinate**, just like my grandmother. _____

6. Aliyah felt **despondent** after her dog died, but talking with her family helped. _____

7. The **mottled** pattern on Sasha's belly makes it easy to tell her apart from the other kittens. _____

8. **Noxious** fumes filled the kitchen, and we hurried outside. _____

9. I was surprised by the **rancor** with which the candidates spoke about one another. _____

10. The **indignant** customer demanded to speak to a manager. _____

11. Dr. Lorenzo has made the **plight** of the rain forests the focus of his career. _____

DAY 8

Vocabulary/Writing

Look closely at the context of each sentence to determine the correct word choice. Then, circle the word that correctly completes each sentence. Use a dictionary to research words if needed.

12. Everyone was able to attend the concert (accept, except) Raymond, who had a previous commitment.
13. Hilda's great-grandparents had (immigrated, emigrated) to the United States from Sweden in the early 1900s.
14. When (its, it's) time to go, we can call the restaurant for an advance reservation.
15. Tokens for the subway (fare, fair) can be purchased in coin-operated machines outside the station.
16. We first brought the towels into the house, (than, then) we folded them and put them away.
17. (There, They're, Their) house on Cherry Street has always been the most majestic old home in all of Gladstone.
18. (Whose, Who's) golf club is this?
19. Manny and Mario have (to, two, too) pet turtles in their room.
20. Mrs. Sherman has been our (principle, principal) for the last two years.
21. When you walk (past, passed) the cafeteria, please check the menu for today's lunch.
22. I am looking for a CD (that, which) has a collection of jazz music.

Select one or two characters, one location, and one event. On a separate piece of paper, use them to write a creative and detailed story.

Characters: talking earthworm, clown, out-of-control robot, princess, teacher, principal

Locations: school, amusement park, boat, airplane, shopping mall, basement

Events: yelling, smelling something unusual, running backward, sneezing, talking while asleep, falling from the sky

FACTOID: Thomas Jefferson spoke six languages.

Geometry/Grammar

DAY 9

Name the congruent angles of each reflection.

1. ∠RQS ≅ ∠____; ∠QRS ≅ ∠____;
   ∠QSR ≅ ∠____

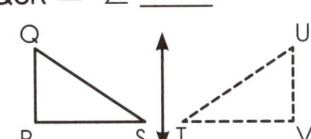

2. ∠____ ≅ ∠____; ∠____ ≅ ∠____;
   ∠____ ≅ ∠____; ∠____ ≅ ∠____;
   ∠____ ≅ ∠____

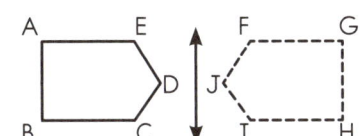

Name the congruent angles of each translation.

3. ∠ABC ≅ ∠____; ∠BCD ≅ ∠____;
   ∠CDA ≅ ∠____; ∠DAB ≅ ∠____

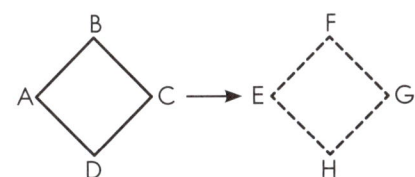

4. ∠____ ≅ ∠____;
   ∠____ ≅ ∠____;
   ∠____ ≅ ∠____;
   ∠____ ≅ ∠____;
   ∠____ ≅ ∠____

Name the congruent angles of each rotation.

5. ∠____ ≅ ∠____; ∠____ ≅ ∠____;
   ∠____ ≅ ∠____

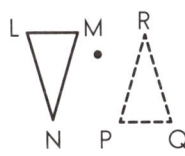

6. ∠____ ≅ ∠____; ∠____ ≅ ∠____;
   ∠____ ≅ ∠____; ∠____ ≅ ∠____

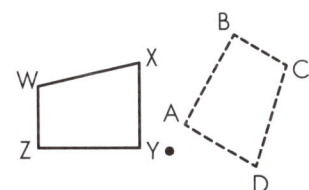

Circle the word that correctly completes each sentence.

7. Gretchen gave Mrs. Cooke a gift and (than, then) told her that she was her favorite teacher.

8. The girls' cross country team win, (that, which) happened in late September, set a new record.

9. (Your, You're) being late for practice cost our team valuable preparation time.

10. The club (that, which) hosted this year's tournament was in Wisconsin.

11. If you don't know where (your, you're) going, how will you know when you get there?

DAY 9

Reading Comprehension

Read the passage. Then, answer the questions.

from *The Call of the Wild* by Jack London

Buck did not read the newspapers, or he would have known that trouble was brewing, not alone for himself, but for every tide-water dog, strong of muscle and with warm, long hair, from Puget Sound to San Diego. Because men, groping in the Arctic darkness, had found a yellow metal, and because steamship and transportation companies were booming the find, thousands of men were rushing into the Northland. These men wanted dogs, and the dogs they wanted were heavy dogs, with strong muscles by which to toil, and furry coats to protect them from the frost.

Buck lived at a big house in the sun-kissed Santa Clara Valley. Judge Miller's place, it was called. It stood back from the road, half hidden among the trees, through which glimpses could be caught of the wide cool veranda that ran around its four sides. The house was approached by gravelled driveways which wound about through wide-spreading lawns and under the interlacing boughs of tall poplars. At the rear things were on even a more spacious scale than at the front. There were great stables, where a dozen grooms and boys held forth, rows of vine-clad servants' cottages, an endless and orderly array of outhouses, long grape arbors, green pastures, orchards, and berry patches. Then there was the pumping plant for the artesian well, and the big cement tank where Judge Miller's boys took their morning plunge and kept cool in the hot afternoon.

And over this great **demesne** Buck ruled. Here he was born, and here he had lived the four years of his life. It was true, there were other dogs. There could not but be other dogs on so vast a place, but they did not count.

12. How does the first paragraph of the selection create suspense?

_____

_____

_____

13. What does the word *demesne* mean? Write a definition using the context of the sentence and then double-check your answer in a dictionary.

_____

14. From whose point of view is the story told? Why is this perspective unusual?

_____

_____

Geometry/Grammar

DAY 10

Draw the rotation of each figure around the point.

1. 180° rotation

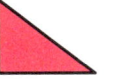

2. 135° rotation

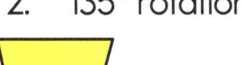

3. 45° rotation

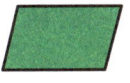

4. 90° counterclockwise rotation

Proper grammar avoids the use of two negatives in the same clause because the result can be confusing. Rewrite each sentence to correct the double negative.

5. Kelly doesn't want no more interruptions.

_____

_____

6. Tracie never did nothing wrong until she broke her mother's favorite vase.

_____

_____

7. Dr. Canberra was born in Argentina, but he never traveled nowhere else once he arrived in the United States.

_____

_____

8. I left home without my umbrella since there is not no chance of rain today.

_____

_____

FACTOID: An adult elephant eats an average of 550 pounds (249.5 kg) of vegetation each day.

DAY 10

Literary Terms/Science

Read each sentence. Write *F* if the sentence is written from the first-person point of view. Write *T* if the sentence is written from the third-person point of view. Then, write a sentence in first person about your favorite sport or hobby.

9. _____ When I saw the size of the gift box, I knew it was the bike I had wanted.
10. _____ Struggling with the humid air, they slowed their pace and rested in a crevice near the rock.
11. _____ The travelers finished packing their bags and headed for the airport.
12. _____ He delivered the newspapers that morning to a total of 96 homes.
13. _____ By morning, I had written the last chapter of my 234-page novel.
14. _____ Despite the low price, I still expect a discount on the draperies.
15. _____ She knows the names of her state senators and representatives.
16. _____

Match each characteristic of metal with its description.

| malleable | ductile | conductor | magnetic | reactivity | alloy |

17. able to be pulled into long wires _____
18. able to be pounded and hammered into different shapes _____
19. a combination of two or more metals _____
20. the ease and speed with which an element combines with other elements and compounds _____
21. a metal that transmits heat and electricity _____
22. the ability to attract other metallic objects _____

CHARACTER CHECK: Make a list of at least three ways you can show tolerance at home and at school. Post the list somewhere visible.

Geometry/Writing

DAY 11

Determine whether each figure or shape has been dilated and write *yes* or *no*. Then, explain your answer by writing *reduced*, *expanded*, or another explanation.

	Dilated?	Explanation
1.	_____	_____
2.	_____	_____
3.	_____	_____
4.	_____	_____
5.	_____	_____
6.	_____	_____
7.	_____	_____
8.	_____	_____

Albert Einstein once said, "Imagination is more important than knowledge." Do you agree or disagree? Write a claim about Einstein's statement. Support your claim with reasons, facts, and examples.

_____
_____
_____
_____
_____

© Carson Dellosa Education

DAY 11

Reading Comprehension

Read the paragraph. Circle the letter of the sentence that states the main idea. Then, underline three supporting details.

The world's tropical rain forests are in great danger. Loggers cut down trees to provide timber and firewood and make room for homes, roads, farms, and factories. Some areas are cleared to mine oil and other valuable minerals. The habitats of thousands of animal and plant species have already vanished. These changes also threaten the way of life for many native residents.

- A. Tropical rain forests contain an incredible amount of plant and animal diversity.
- B. Tropical rain forests are in great danger.
- C. Tropical rain forests are located near the equator.

Read the passage. Then, answer the questions.

The U.S. Government

The U.S. government consists of three separate branches: executive, legislative, and judicial. The president, vice president, and the cabinet of advisors represent the executive branch. The president, elected by the people, chooses the cabinet, subject to Senate approval. The Senate and House of Representatives form the U.S. Congress in the legislative branch. Each state elects two senators. Senators' six-year terms are staggered so that only one-third of the Senate is elected every two years. Each state also elects a designated number of representatives, determined by state population. The House of Representatives contains 435 members. All representatives are elected every two years. The third branch of the U.S. government is the judicial branch, which consists of courts of law throughout the nation. The highest court is the Supreme Court, containing nine justices. When a justice's seat opens, the president nominates a candidate who must be approved by the Senate.

9. What is the main idea of this passage?
    - A. The Senate approves the president's cabinet choices.
    - B. The president and members of Congress are elected.
    - C. The U.S. government contains three separate branches.

10. Which offices form the executive branch? _____

11. Which groups represent the U.S. Congress? _____

> **FACTOID:** The first successful helicopter flight occurred in 1906. Its time off the ground was 20 seconds.

Geometry/Parts of Speech

DAY 12

Use each scale factor to determine whether the dilation is an enlargement or a reduction.

1. SF = $\frac{1}{2}$ _____
2. SF = 120% _____
3. SF = $\frac{8}{9}$ _____
4. SF = 32% _____
5. SF = 4 _____
6. SF = $\frac{2}{3}$ _____
7. SF = 247% _____
8. SF = 8 _____

Find the scale factor in each dilation.

9.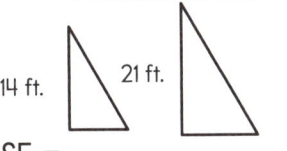

   SF = _____

10. SF = _____

11. 14 ft.   21 ft.

    SF = _____

12. 4 mm   8 mm

    SF = _____

Each sentence contains a shift in verb voice or mood. Rewrite it correctly on the line to correct the error.

13. When Ana Maria opened her book, a stain was seen on the page.
    _____

14. If I was you, I would have left the performance during intermission.
    _____

15. Pack your lunch, and then you should let the dog out.
    _____

16. Kiku was elected class president, and changes were made throughout the year in the school.
    _____

17. If we had won the game, we will go out to celebrate afterward.
    _____

DAY 12

Read the passage. Then, answer the questions.

Halley's Comet

Halley's Comet was named for its discoverer, astronomer Edmond Halley. Halley had theorized that comets were natural **phenomena** of the solar system that traveled in orbits around the sun. He maintained that one specific comet would take 76 years to complete its orbit. After researching sightings in the years 1531, 1607, and 1682, Halley predicted that the comet would return in 1758. His prediction was accurate, and the comet was named in his honor, 16 years after his death. Since that time, Halley's Comet has made regular visits to Earth's orbit about every 76 years. Various forces combine to keep the orbit consistent. However, the gravitational pull of the planets sometimes changes the orbital period. There have been times when the comet's orbit has taken as long as 79 years.

Astronomers have researched the composition of comets. In 1985, the spacecraft *Giotto* was launched to photograph Halley's Comet as it passed Earth. The pictures were taken from 370 miles (600 km) away, the closest distance at which the comet has been monitored. *Giotto* sent valuable data to astronomers. Measurements showed that the comet's nucleus is approximately 9 miles (15 km) in diameter. The dark and porous nucleus is composed of dust that remained after ice changed into a gaseous state. Halley's Comet is scheduled to pass by Earth again in 2061.

18. Which of the following reasons makes Halley's Comet the best-known comet?
    A. the size of its nucleus
    B. its fairly regular orbital pattern
    C. its composition of ice turned to dust
    D. its beauty

19. How often does Halley's Comet pass by Earth?
    A. approximately every 76 years
    B. usually every 89 years
    C. cannot be predicted
    D. once every other century

20. What is the approximate size of the nucleus of Halley's Comet? _____

21. Which of the following best defines the word *phenomena*?
    A. a comet with a predictable orbit
    B. observable, unusual facts or events
    C. routine conditioning
    D. beyond expectation

22. What causes the orbit of Halley's Comet to vary slightly in duration?
    _____

FITNESS FLASH: Jog in place for 30 seconds.

* See page ii.

Algebra/Language Arts

DAY 13

The rate of change, or *slope*, of a function can be found in different ways. When a function is shown as an equation, the slope is the absolute value of the coefficient of x. When a function is shown as a graph, choose two points on the line and use them to calculate the rate of change using the equation $\frac{y_2 - y_1}{x_2 - x_1}$. For each pair of functions below, write *equation*, *graph*, or *equal* to tell which has the greater slope.

EXAMPLE: $y = -2x + 3$ or

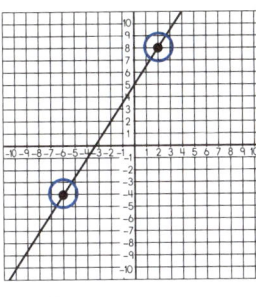

The slope is |–2|, or 2.

The rate of change is $\frac{8 - (-4)}{2 - (-6)} = \frac{12}{8} = \frac{3}{2}$.

Because 2 is greater than $\frac{3}{2}$, the function represented by the equation has the greater rate of change.

1. $y = \frac{1}{2}x - 2$ or

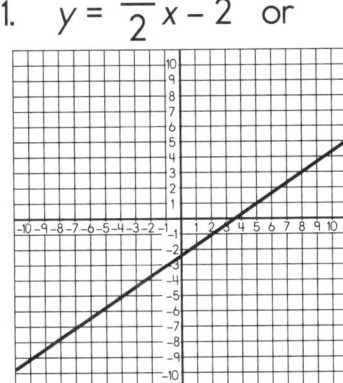

_____

2. $y = -6x + 1$ or

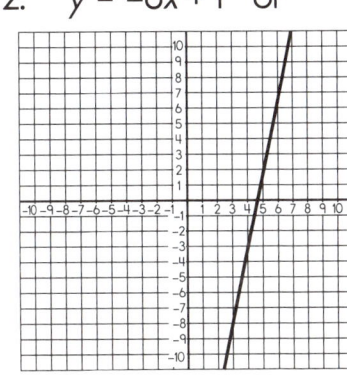

_____

3. $y = 3x - 2$ or

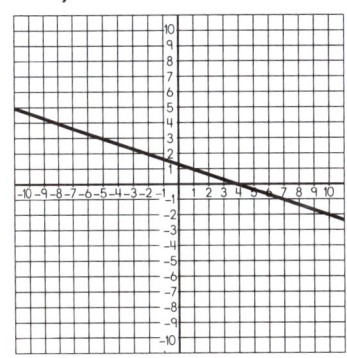

_____

Read the passage. Draw three lines under each letter that should be capitalized.

Spanish Exploration

Spain made attempts to build settlements in florida, but all were failures. Then, king phillip II commissioned Pedro Menendez de Aviles to colonize Florida and drive out any pirates or settlers from other nations.

When menendez arrived in florida in 1565, he, his soldiers, and 500 colonists landed near the american indian village of seloy. Menendez and his men built a fort with the help of some american indians and named the new settlement st. augustine.

DAY 13

Science/Character Development

Organize the words from the word bank using the outline below.

cows	mammals	frogs	salamanders	amphibians
animals	cardinals	lions	birds	robins
crocodiles	vertebrates	reptiles	snakes	

I. _____
A. _____
1. _____
   a. _____
   b. _____
2. _____
   a. _____
   b. _____
3. _____
   a. _____
   b. _____
4. _____
   a. _____
   b. _____

A Persevering Attitude

Perseverance means *the action of continuing, even if a task is difficult.* Think about perseverance. When have you seen people demonstrating this quality? What were they doing? What were they hoping to accomplish? Read the situations below. Select one situation. Then, draw a three-panel comic strip showing the before, during, and after. Be sure to include a caption for each panel to describe your persevering attitude.

- You have recently adopted a puppy. The puppy is very energetic and playful. At first, its actions are cute; however, as the puppy grows, you realize that the puppy needs to be trained. You know that teaching the puppy good habits will take perseverance on your part.

- You just found a great summer camp that offers all of the activities that you most enjoy. Your best friend is going, and you want to go too. Your family informs you that you will need to pay for some of the expenses. It is a lot of money to save in a short period of time, but you decide to persevere and make the effort to save the necessary money.

FACTOID: The word *salary* comes from the Latin word *sal*, which means *salt*. Roman soldiers were paid an allowance to buy salt.

Data Analysis — DAY 14

A *frequency table* shows how often values appear in a data set. *Frequency* describes how many times a value appears. *Cumulative frequency* describes the sum of all frequencies to that point. *Relative frequency* compares the frequency of each number in the category with the total number. Complete the charts with the missing numbers. Give answers in simplest form. Then, answer the questions.

The heights of students in inches are as follows: 66, 68, 65, 70, 67, 64, 70, 64, 66, 70, 72, 71, 69, 69, 64, 67, 63, 67, 71, 63, 68, 67, 65, 69, 65, 67, 66, 68, 64, and 69.

Height Range	Frequency	Cumulative Frequency	Relative Frequency
63–64	6	6	$\frac{1}{5}$
65–66	6	12	$\frac{1}{5}$
1. 67–68	8	20	$\frac{4}{15}$
2. 69–70	7	27	$\frac{7}{30}$
3. 71–72	3	30	$\frac{1}{10}$

4. At what height are most students? _____ 67–68
5. How many students were measured? _____ 30

One die was rolled with the following results: 6, 5, 4, 4, 5, 6, 1, 2, 1, 6, 4, 3, 3, 3, 4, 2, 2, 5, 6, 4, 1, 2, 4, 3, 5, 5, 3, 3, 4, and 2.

Roll	Frequency	Cumulative Frequency	Relative Frequency
6. 1	3	3	$\frac{1}{10}$
7. 2	5	8	$\frac{1}{6}$
8. 3	6	14	$\frac{1}{5}$
9. 4	7	21	$\frac{7}{30}$
10. 5	5	26	$\frac{1}{6}$
11. 6	4	30	$\frac{2}{15}$

12. How many times was the die rolled? _____ 30
13. Which number was rolled most frequently? _____ 4

DAY 14

Literary Terms/Science

Persuasive writing is meant to influence the reader to agree with a belief, a position, or a course of action. Expository writing provides information or explains something that may be difficult to understand. Narrative writing describes an event or tells a story.

Read each description. Write P for persuasive, E for expository, or N for narrative to indicate the type of writing.

14. _____ a story about martians in a science fiction magazine
15. _____ the history of how Thomas Edison invented the lightbulb
16. _____ a letter published in a newspaper that encourages voters to support arts education in schools

Write the word from the word bank that matches each description.

| gasohol | geothermal | hydroelectric | solar |
| nuclear | biomass | wind | |

17. _____ energy produced by atomic reactions
18. _____ energy collected from the sun's radiation
19. _____ energy that produces electricity using the flow of water
20. _____ energy that turns a windmill to pump water or produce electricity
21. _____ energy produced by the heat beneath Earth's surface
22. _____ energy produced from burning organic materials, such as wood
23. _____ fuel produced when plants are changed into alcohol and then mixed with gasoline

FITNESS FLASH: Do 10 jumping jacks.

* See page ii.

Measurement/Vocabulary

DAY 15

Solve each problem using a formula from the box. Use 3.14 for π. Round answers to the nearest hundredth.

Cylinder: $V = \pi r^2 h$ Cone: $V = \frac{1}{3}\pi r^2 h$ Sphere: $V = \frac{4}{3}\pi r^3$

1. Maddie has a mailing cylinder for posters that measures 24 inches long and 4 inches in diameter. What is the volume of the tube?

    _____ in.³

2. A basketball has a diameter of 9.4 inches. What is the volume of the basketball?

    _____ in.³

3. A cone-shaped party hat is 25 cm tall and has a diameter of 21 cm. What is the volume of the party hat?

    _____ cm³

4. Glass A measures 84 mm in diameter and 175 mm tall. Glass B measures 96 mm in diameter and 125 mm tall. Which glass holds more liquid? How much more?

    Glass _____ holds _____ mm³ more liquid than Glass _____.

Use the context of each sentence to help you determine the meaning of the underlined word. Write the meaning on the line. Then, look up the word in a print or online dictionary to double-check the definition.

5. We hoped to go to the beach for a vacation this summer, but after my stepdad started a new job, it just wasn't feasible.

    _____

6. Kirsten decided to juxtapose several photographs in a collage she created for Mr. Ruben's art class.

    _____

7. A pungent odor filled the room when Mrs. Petrelli dropped the eggs.

    _____

8. As I read the story, I noticed a motif of mirrors appearing repeatedly.

    _____

DAY 15

Reading Comprehension

Read the passage. Then, answer the questions.

Sue Hendrickson

As a child, Sue Hendrickson loved to dig and was always searching for treasures. In the mid-1970s, Hendrickson went hiking with friends to an amber mine. A miner showed Hendrickson a piece of amber with a 23-million-year-old insect trapped inside. This began her lifelong search for **fossils**.

Hendrickson began her career as an archaeologist by digging for bones in the deserts of Peru. She worked with a group of archaeologists who searched for bones of water animals in land that was once under the sea. She helped discover whale, dolphin, and seal bones hundreds of miles from existing water.

In 1990, Hendrickson journeyed to South Dakota with an archaeological team that was digging for dinosaur bones. When the team's truck had a flat tire, the other scientists left to get the tire fixed. But, Hendrickson and her dog stayed behind and went for a walk. She wanted to examine some cliffs that they had not had time to explore.

Hendrickson saw some bones on the ground and looked up. Preserved in the sandstone cliff above her was an enormous dinosaur skeleton! The group immediately began to work on the find. They uncovered the largest, most complete *Tyrannosaurus rex* skeleton ever found. The team named the *T. rex* Sue, after its discoverer.

This was not Sue Hendrickson's only adventure. Two years later, she went with other scientists to explore a Spanish trading ship that sank in 1600. They uncovered huge stone jars, 100 skeletons, and more than 400 gold and silver coins at the shipwreck.

9. Which of the following words best describes Sue Hendrickson?
   A. stern   B. adventurous   C. quiet   D. funny

10. What does the word *fossil* mean? _____

11. In what year did Hendrickson discover the *T. rex* skeleton? _____

12. How did Hendrickson find the T. rex bones?
    A. She was digging in the earth with scientists when they found the skeleton.
    B. Her dog found the bones and ran back to get her.
    C. She went for a walk while she was waiting for a flat tire to be fixed.

13. With an adult's help, watch a video interview with Sue Hendrickson that you find online. What are the advantages of using more than one type of media to research and learn about a topic? Use a separate sheet of paper to write your response.

Data Analysis/Language Arts

DAY 16

A *stem-and-leaf plot* is one way to organize a set of data. In a stem-and-leaf plot, the greatest place value common to a group of numbers is used for the stem. The lower place values form the leaves. For example, if a set of data contained the numbers 11, 14, 15, and 16, the stem and leaf plot would look like this: 1 | 1, 4, 5, 6.

1. Write two situations in which you might want to use a stem-and-leaf plot to organize numbers. _____
_____

Use the stem-and-leaf plot to answer the questions.

Stem	Leaf
4	6, 8
5	2, 8, 9
6	1, 2, 5, 5
7	3, 4, 4

2. List the numbers in the stem. _____

3. How many numbers have stem 6? _____

4. Name the low number and the high number. _____

5. What is the range? _____

Add commas where they are needed in each sentence. Write *A* if the commas separate an appositive or appositive phrase, *D* for a direct address, or *P* for a parenthetical expression.

6. _____ The answer of course is 44.
7. _____ Bridget the tallest girl on the team is a great tennis player.
8. _____ If you wait Justin we will go with you.
9. _____ Button stop scratching the cushions.
10. _____ Nadia please call your brother on the phone.
11. _____ I told you Shay not to wait too long to start your project.
12. _____ Mrs. Ramirez the hardest seventh-grade English teacher gave me an A on my essay.

DAY 16

Reading Comprehension/Science

Read each effect. Then, write a possible cause.

Cause	Effect
13. _____	A. Looking haggard, Melissa arrived late for biology class.
14. _____	B. Thousands of people, some in red and blue caps, others in green and white, gathered in the large arena.
15. _____	C. The Canadian gymnast performed her best balance beam routine to win an Olympic gold medal.
16. _____	D. Crying, Jackie clutched her crimson purse and began the long walk home.
17. _____	E. Dr. Peoples asked the patient to go to the third floor for a chest X-ray.

A *physical change* occurs with force, such as motion, temperature, or pressure. For example, when energy (heat) is added to ice, it melts. The state of matter has changed, but the chemical composition remains the same. When a *chemical change* occurs an object's molecules change. A new substance with a different chemical makeup is formed. For example, when iron rusts, change occurs over a long period of time. Iron molecules combine with oxygen to become iron oxide.

Identify each change as a physical change or a chemical change.

18. water freezing _____
19. wood burning _____
20. frying an egg _____
21. glass breaking _____
22. food spoiling _____

CHARACTER CHECK: Draw a comic strip showing a character who demonstrates determination.

Geometry/Writing

DAY 17

Find the distance between each of the points given using the Pythagorean theorem. Round answers to the nearest hundredth.

1.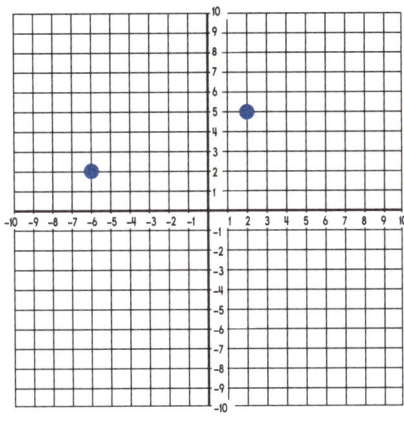

_____

2.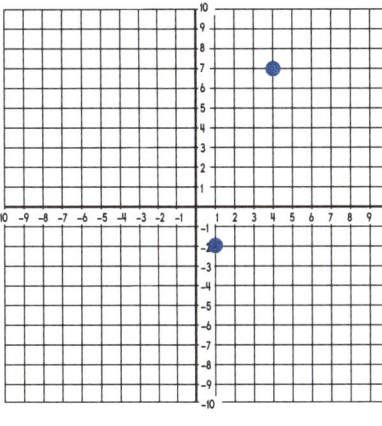

_____

3.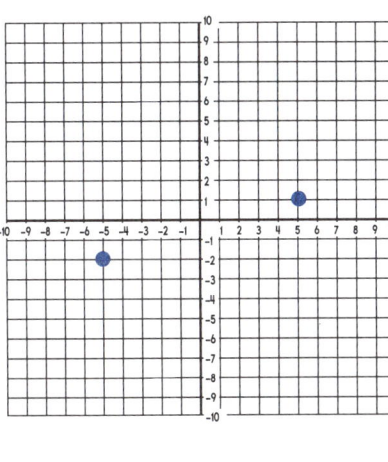

_____

4.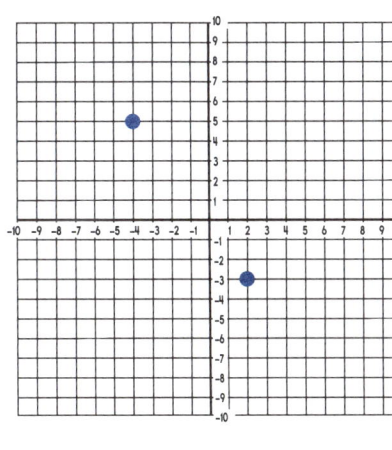

_____

Write a short talk for elementary school students about how to budget your time wisely. Include specific facts and examples. Use a separate sheet of paper if you need more space for your talk.

_____

_____

_____

_____

_____

DAY 17

Language Arts/Fitness

Many nonfiction books contain features that convey or organize information in different ways for the reader. Write each book feature from the word bank next to its definition.

> table of contents   index   glossary   pictures
> title page   caption   bibliography

5. _____ an alphabetical list of special terms and their definitions found in the back of a book

6. _____ a list of reference books and articles found in the back of the book

7. _____ an alphabetical list at the back of the book that includes people, places, key words, or topics in the book, with page numbers for quick reference

8. _____ a description or explanation for a photograph or illustration

9. _____ a page at the front of the book listing the book title and author, and usually the publisher

10. _____ illustrations or photographs

11. _____ a list of chapters and corresponding page numbers found at the front of the book

Power Walking

Power walking is a great exercise for building endurance. Set a time or distance goal for your first power walk. Then, think of some places where you can walk. Plan to walk with a friend, parent, or guardian in your neighborhood, on a trail at a local park, or at a mall. Set monthly goals to increase your walking time or distance. Track your progress and before you know it, you will be walking miles and improving your endurance and overall fitness!

FITNESS FLASH: Hop on your left foot 10 times.

* See page ii.

Algebra/Language Arts

DAY 18

To solve a system of equations, substitute one equation for y in the other equation. Then, solve for x. Finally, substitute the value of x in one of the equations to solve for y. Solve each system of equations. Give the values for x and y as an ordered pair.

1. $y = 2x$
   $y = x + 4$

2. $y = x - 5$
   $y = 2x + 1$

3. $y = 4x - 5$
   $y = 2x + 3$

4. $y = 5x - 14$
   $y = x + 10$

5. $y = -2x + 1$
   $y = 4x - 3$

6. $y = x + 7$
   $y = -4x - 2$

Read each sentence. Add semicolons, commas, and colons as needed.

7. Mr. Cole decided to meet with Ms. Grayson Ben's math teacher Mr. Robbins his science teacher and Mrs. Abernathy his English teacher.

8. Raymond Webb just graduated from college he plans to attend law school.

9. The first rule in this class respect other students' rights.

10. The parent company left its main facility open but closed plants in Greensboro North Carolina Jacksonville Florida and Harrisburg Pennsylvania.

11. Will Rogers made this comment on attitude "Don't let yesterday use up too much of today."

12. Alyson accepted the job as a telemarketer for one reason she wanted to work at home while Amy was a baby.

13. Have you ever heard the saying "You can't afford the luxury of a negative thought"?

14. Grace did well in three subjects therefore she will have a high average at the end of the semester.

DAY 18

Read the passage. Then, answer the questions.

The Tang Dynasty

For many years, China was governed by a series of dynasties, or rulers from the same families. The Tang Dynasty, which ruled from about AD 618 to 907, is considered to have been one of the most prosperous dynasties. This period is referred to as China's Golden Age. The arts, including theater, dance, sculpting, and painting, were all valued and very popular during this time. More than one million people lived in the capital city of Chang'an. Farmers were allowed to own land, although this later changed. People who wanted to work in the government had to pass a difficult exam. Only the smartest and most educated people could serve as government officials. The Tang Dynasty charged taxes per individual in a family instead of by property owned. So, the government conducted a very accurate census to determine the empire's population, and households paid taxes on grain and cloth. Trade inside China and to other countries also flourished because new roads and canals built by the previous Sui Dynasty made travel easier. Today, the period ruled by the Tang Dynasty is remembered as a time of great cultural achievement.

15. What is the main idea of this passage?
    A. The Tang government taxed grain and cloth.
    B. The Tang Dynasty lasted for nearly 300 years.
    C. The Tang Dynasty ruled during a period of great cultural achievement.

16. What artistic activities were popular during the Tang Dynasty? _____

17. How did people become government officials? _____

18. Why did the government conduct a census? _____

19. Why did trade during the Tang Dynasty flourish? _____

FACTOID: One out of every two people in the world is under the age of 25.

Fractions & Decimals/Grammar

DAY 19

Compare using <, >, or =.

1. $\sqrt{\frac{1}{9}}$ _____ $\frac{1}{4}$
2. $\frac{4}{7}$ _____ $\sqrt{3}$
3. $\sqrt{50}$ _____ $\sqrt[3]{125}$

4. 2.5 _____ $\sqrt{5}$
5. $\sqrt{11}$ _____ 3
6. 5 _____ $\sqrt[3]{45}$

7. $\sqrt{\frac{4}{49}}$ _____ $\frac{3}{5}$
8. $\sqrt{600}$ _____ 6^2
9. 100 _____ $\sqrt[3]{10^6}$

Read the passage. Add punctuation and correct any other errors as necessary.

The origin of the ice-cream cone has been controversial for several centuries some historians claim that the first paper cone came from France while others maintain that metal cones were used in Germany. Still other people say that an Italian genius introduced the first ice-cream cone.

Ice cream was referred to in Europe as iced pudding and the cones were called wafers. Eating establishments often served the wafers after a meal to soothe digestion. But, once chefs rolled the wafers into funnels the cones could be filled with anything including ice cream.

However many Americans believe that the first edible ice-cream cone was created in the United States. Italo Marchiony who emigrated from Italy created edible cones and sold them from pushcarts in the streets of New York City for a penny each. Marchiony eventually patented his invention in 1903.

DAY 19

Vocabulary/Language Arts

Choose the word or the phrase in each group that does not belong. Then, explain your selection.

10. A. central   B. cirrus
    C. stratus   D. cumulus
    _____

11. A. pulley   B. wedge
    C. crate   D. screw
    _____

12. A. oxygen   B. hydrogen
    C. helium   D. calcium
    _____

13. A. skeletal B. temperature
    C. muscular D. circulatory
    _____

14. A. artery   B. membrane
    C. ribosome D. mitochondrion
    _____

Create a glossary for a book about superheroes. What words might be included in such a glossary? Be creative. Invent new words or special definitions. Create at least 20 entries for your superhero glossary. Use a separate sheet of paper if needed.

_____
_____
_____
_____

FITNESS FLASH: Hop on your right foot for 30 seconds.

* See page ii.

Problem Solving/Grammar

DAY 20

Set up a system of equations to solve each word problem.

1. Stella has 63 coins. The coins are a mixture of quarters and dimes. She has a total of $10.80. How many quarters and how many dimes does Stella have?

   Equation 1: _____   Equation 2: _____

   Stella has _____ quarters and _____ dimes.

2. Last Saturday, 1,750 people attended an event at Fairway Gardens. The admission fee was $3.50 for children and $8.00 for adults. If the total amount of money collected at the event was $9,860, how many children and how many adults attended the event?

   Equation 1: _____   Equation 2: _____

   _____ adults and _____ children attended the event.

Read each pair of sentences. Circle the letter of the sentence that contains an error.

3. A. The dance was a lot of fun.
   B. Me and my friend got home late.

4. A. She did good on the exam.
   B. My dad works many hours.

5. A. Is your bicycle broke?
   B. My ankle looks like it is swollen.

6. A. I don't want no homework.
   B. Did you mean to say that?

7. A. Sam and I walked to the store.
   B. She changed it's tire.

8. A. Trenton spread alot of jam on the bread.
   B. Can you wait a minute?

9. A. The ocean was so choppy.
   B. There car would not start.

10. A. He played bad.
    B. The tennis game had no winner.

DAY 20

Critical Thinking/Social Studies

Ellen, Julie, Ben, and Dante are athletes. Each person participates in a different sport: tennis, golf, skating, and track. All four athletes are sitting at a square table. Use the information below and deductive reasoning to determine each person's sport and where each athlete is sitting.

- The runner sits across from Dante.
- The tennis player sits on Julie's right.
- Dante and Julie sit next to each other.
- A man sits to the left of the runner.
- The skater sits to the left of the tennis player.

Write the name of each Renaissance figure next to his description.

> Miguel de Cervantes
> John Milton
> Leonardo da Vinci
> Michelangelo
> Nicolaus Copernicus
> Galileo Galilei
> Johannes Gutenberg

11. _____ invented the mechanical printing press.

12. _____ was a novelist, poet, and playwright whose book, *Don Quixote*, is considered to be the first modern novel.

13. _____ was a painter, sculptor, architect, and engineer who sculpted *David* and painted the ceiling of the Sistine Chapel.

14. _____ was a physicist, mathematician, and astronomer known for his belief that the sun was the center of the universe.

15. _____ was a scientist, artist, inventor, and mathematician whose most famous painting is the *Mona Lisa*.

16. _____ was a poet and author of *Paradise Lost*.

17. _____ was the first astronomer to argue that Earth is not the center of the universe.

CHARACTER CHECK: Write five things that you are grateful for.

Science Experiment

BONUS

Erosion

Wind, water, and ice can shape and reshape various landforms on the earth's surface. Over time, sand dunes recede, boulders break into sand, and jagged mountains become gently rolling hills. Erosion is the movement of rock and soil from one area to another area on the earth's surface.

Materials:
- small plastic container
- cup of potting soil
- modeling clay
- measuring teaspoon
- cup of sand
- cup of water
- ice cube

Procedure:
Pour the sand into the plastic container. Gently blow on the sand. What happened? This resembles how wind affects sand. Wind picks up sand from one place and moves it to a different place. This is called *wind erosion*. Carefully pour the sand back into the cup.

Pour the soil into the plastic container. Firmly pack the soil into the bottom of the container. Carefully pour a small river of water down the middle of the soil. Move the cup in a back-and-forth motion while pouring until the cup is empty. What did the water do to the soil? Over time, water can have the same effect on rock. This is called *water erosion*. Carefully pour the soil back into the cup.

Press the modeling clay into the bottom of the plastic container. Sprinkle 1 teaspoon (5 mL) of sand on top of the clay. Rub the ice cube over the sand. What happened to the sand? What happened to the clay? As glaciers move slowly over land, they pick up rocks that scrape the land and leave deep scratches. This is called *ice erosion*.

Complete the following sentences.

1. Blowing _____ can move dirt and sand from one area to another.

2. As _____ flows in rivers and other bodies of water, it picks up pebbles and sand along the bottom and the sides.

3. The hard _____ of glaciers scrapes across the land, picking up dirt and boulders along the way.

© Carson Dellosa Education

Science Experiment

BONUS

Examining the Effects of Acid Rain

Acid rain is a serious environmental issue. Acid rain can destroy forests, harm wildlife, and erode buildings, monuments, and statues. Acid rain is produced when water vapor in the air reacts with sulfur dioxide and nitrogen oxide, which in turn produces sulfuric acid and nitric acid. These chemicals fall to the earth in the form of precipitation, or acid rain. The chemicals are pollutants that come from burning fossil fuels such as coal and gasoline. In this experiment, students will discover how acid rain affects plants.

Materials:
- 4 index cards
- 4 identical potted plants
- tap water
- bottled water
- vinegar
- orange juice
- measuring cups

Procedure:
Use the index cards to label the plants as follows: *Plant 1: Tap Water, Plant 2: Bottled Water, Plant 3: Tap Water and Vinegar, Plant 4: Tap Water and Orange Juice.*

Water all of the plants with the same amount of liquid at the same time. Give plant 1 tap water, plant 2 bottled water, and plant 3 a 1:1 mixture of tap water and vinegar. For example, add 1/4 cup (59 mL) of vinegar to 1/4 cup (59 mL) of tap water. Then, give plant 4 a 1:1 mixture of tap water and orange juice.

Place the plants near a window or in a well-lit area so that they receive the same amount of light. How does each plant look? Record your observations in the chart. Then, use what you have learned to complete the conclusion below.

	Week 1	Week 2	Week 3	Week 4
Plant 1				
Plant 2				
Plant 3				
Plant 4				

The _____ and _____ mixtures are similar to acid rain in how they affect plants. _____ contains an acid called *citric acid*. _____ is an acid, too. These two substances mixed with water duplicate the effects of acid rain on the plants. The acids weaken the plants, and when the plants are not given fresh water, they die.

Social Studies Activity

BONUS

Budgeting

The U.S. federal government receives money from taxes and decides how to spend it. With many costs and programs to fund, it is often difficult to decide how much to spend on each item. The government frequently borrows money to pay for all of these costs and programs. This borrowed money becomes the national debt.

Below is a list of things you might want to buy or do. Each item on the list has a price range. Assume that the more money you spend, the better product or service you will receive. (Consumer note: This is not always true, but for this activity, pretend it is.) You have only $75 to spend, but you want to do as much as you can with it. You do have some extra money in your savings account, and your brother said that he would also lend you some money.

You must decide which items or services you will buy and how much you will spend on each. Try not to borrow from your savings or your brother because you will go into debt. Circle your choices and write what you chose to spend on each. At the bottom of the page, show your total spent. Then, explain why you chose to purchase each item.

_____	gift for Mom ($10–$25)	_____	helmet and pads for scooter ($15–$20)
_____	cell phone ($5–$40)		
_____	cell phone service ($25–$38)	_____	book ($7–$16)
		_____	guitar ($31–$50)
_____	video game ($15–$33)	_____	guitar lessons ($5–$9)
_____	shoes ($29–$50)	_____	pizza ($6–$12)
_____	scooter ($22–$48)	_____	movie ticket ($2–$8)

Total Spent: _____

Why did you choose to purchase each item? _____

_____

_____

Visit www.treasurydirect.gov/kids/kids.htm to learn more about the history of the U.S. national debt. On a separate sheet of paper, write several paragraphs comparing and contrasting personal debt (the kind you'd have if you borrowed money from your brother) with the national debt.

BONUS

Social Studies Activity

Comparing Countries

For the countries below, research and write one fact for each category.

	Argentina	Finland	Cambodia
Population			
Capital City			
Official Language(s)			
Type of Government			
Products			

Social Studies Activity

BONUS

Women's Suffrage Movement

As the 20th century rolled in, women were still unable to vote in the United States. They held jobs, raised families, participated in politics, and kept the country going during World War I. But they were not allowed to help elect the nation's leaders.

Elizabeth Cady Stanton was a loud voice in the women's suffrage, or voting rights, movement. She ran for Congress in 1866. Although she could not vote at that time, she could run for office. Stanton received only 24 votes. This defeat did not stop her. Susan B. Anthony also worked tirelessly to win women the right to vote. She traveled back and forth across the country giving speeches.

Elizabeth Cady Stanton and Susan B. Anthony never gave up. Finally, on August 18, 1920, the 19th amendment was ratified. It granted American women the right to vote.

Imagine that you will give a speech in support of women's suffrage. Answer the questions to plan your speech. You may need to do some background research as well.

Circle your choices.

1. You are going to imagine that you are
    A. Susan B. Anthony.
    B. Elizabeth Cady Stanton.
    C. a politician in 1919 who needs votes.

2. You are going to write your speech about
    A. why women should have the right to vote.
    B. how women's suffrage will help the country.
    C. your own feelings and experiences.

3. You would like the people who hear your speech to
    A. agree with your point of view.
    B. join the movement.
    C. tell others about the movement.

Finish each sentence. Write your speech on a separate sheet of paper.

4. The main reason I am giving a speech about women's suffrage is _____
_____ .

5. I have spoken about women's rights _____ times before.

6. One detail I will use in my speech is _____
_____ .

BONUS

Outdoor Extension Activities

Take It Outside!

With the assistance of a family member, plan a family trip to a special summer event. Discuss the possible costs, such as the cost of fuel, food, entrance, and parking. Make a list of these expenses. Then, project the costs for each item and the total cost for the family trip. On the day of the event, review the budget with your family. Keep all receipts as money is spent. Add all receipts at the end of the day. How much was spent? Did you stay on budget? Did you go over or under budget? Share the results with your family.

Find a place in your community that sells alternative energy sources. Call ahead to schedule a visit. Take a pen and a notebook with you and interview a salesperson regarding the benefits of using the alternative energy source. Ask for brochures that explain the apparatus or the facility's function and purpose. After the interview, review your notes and the brochures. Then, create a 30-second commercial about the benefits of using this alternative energy source. Send a thank-you letter to the person you interviewed and describe what you learned.

With an adult, visit an area in your community where people exercise outdoors. With a pen and a notebook, list the various activities that you see people doing, such as running, cycling, walking, or kayaking. Then, tally the number of people doing each activity. At the end of one hour, count the tally marks. Determine how many people you saw exercising and the percentages for each form of exercise observed. Which form of exercise had the highest percentage? Which had the lowest?

Section I

Day 1/Page 3: 1. 496 ft.²; 2. 346 mm²; 3. 880 in.²; 4. 168 cm³; 5. 960 m³; 6. 420 yd.³; Students should capitalize the words in green: **American** pioneers followed several routes on their journeys west. Pioneers from **New England** traveled across **New York** on the **Mohawk Trail**. Another route led through the **Cumberland Gap**, a natural pass in the **Appalachian Mountains** that ends near the borders of **Kentucky**, **Tennessee**, and **Virginia**. **The** first groups of settlers crossing the **Appalachian Mountains** in the late 1700s and early 1800s followed these early trails. The popular **Conestoga** wagon, which originated in **Pennsylvania** and was probably introduced by **Mennonite German** settlers, carried many pioneers migrating southward through the **Great Appalachian Valley** along the **Great Wagon Road**.; 7. D; 8. B; 9. B; 10. D; 11. A; 12. F; 13. E; 14. G; 15. A; 16. C; 17. B; 18. D

Day 2/Page 5: 1. quadrilateral; 2. quadrilateral; 3. rectangle; 4. triangle; 5. Lila has always felt competitive with her intelligent, charming, athletic older sister.; 6. The heavy, leather-bound antique dictionary had been passed down for four generations.; 7. The nervous, expectant mother was sure that her baby would arrive before morning.; 8. The Goldsteins had driven hundreds of miles to see the majestic, towering redwood trees.; 9. Nazir picked nearly a bushel of juicy, red apples.; 10. It seemed only fitting that Monday began as a chilly, gray, drizzly day.; 11. The clear, blue water seemed to beckon to Rafael.; 12. The brown, spotted frog jumped onto a rock and sat there motionless all morning.; 13. Juice from the plump, ripe strawberries dribbled down Katrina's chin.; 14. The eager, excited fans cheered when the players jogged onto the field.; 15. N; 16. P; 17. N; 18. N; 19. P; 20. P; 21. P; 22. P; 23. C; 24. firsthand information about an event from the view of someone who was present when the event happened; 25. information from primary sources; 26. Answers will vary.

Day 3/Page 7: 1. $\frac{19}{40}$ cups of broth per serving; 2. $\frac{50\frac{4}{5}}{4} = \frac{m}{1}$, $12\frac{7}{10}$ miles per hour; 3. $\frac{124\frac{7}{8}}{25} = \frac{g}{1}$, $4\frac{199}{200}$ gallons per minute; 4.–10. Letters in green should be circled. 4. facilitate, verb, to make something easier; 5. **mez**zanine, noun, the lowest balcony in a theater; 6. **ac**complice, noun, someone associated with another, especially in wrongdoing; 7. **pro**mulgate, verb, to make an idea known to many people; 8. **patri**arch, noun, a man who controls a family, group, or government; 9. **con**fiscate, verb, to take away, 10. **util**itarian, adjective, necessary; 11. B; 12. B; 13. The main idea of the selection is that honeybees have a special relationship with flowers. The second paragraph provides details about how bees communicate the location of flowers.

Day 4/Page 9:

x	1	2	3	4	5
y	3	6	9	12	15

$k = 3$

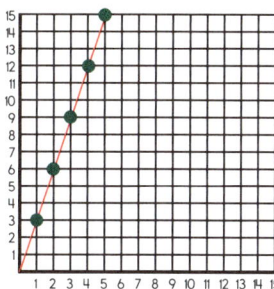

The graph is a straight line.; 1. h; 2. f; 3. a; 4. c; 5. g; 6. b; 7. d; 8. e; 9. bulldozer; 10. doze; 11. perilous; 12. recipe; 13. breakfast; 14. charcoal; Students' writing will vary.

Day 5/Page 11: 1. 8 m; 2. 15 cm; 3. 28 m; 4. 32 in.; 5. $\frac{1}{6}$; 6. $\frac{1}{3}$; 7. $\frac{1}{2}$; 8. $\frac{5}{6}$; 9. $\frac{1}{2}$; 10. $\frac{2}{3}$; 11. A; 12. B; 13. B; 14. B; 15. A; 16. A

Day 6/Page 13: 1. Charley's class; 2. Charley; 3. 4 out of 25, or about 1 in 6; 4. about 10; 5.–11. Students should underline the words in green twice: 5. **is**, novel → *The Book Thief*; 6. **is**, author → Charles Dickens; 7. **is**, wizard → One; 8. **is**, tale → story; 9. **is**, book → *Harry Potter and the Sorcerer's Stone*; 10. **is**, book → *The Westing Game*; 11. **are**, novels → *Animal Farm* and *1984*; 12. They wanted each state to have the same number of representatives so that less-populated states would have as much say as more-populated states.; 13. They would have more votes than the smaller states.; 14. when two sides make concessions to reach an agreement; 15.–16. Answers will vary.

Day 7/Page 15: 1. ∠S and ∠Z, ∠T and ∠Y; 2. ∠V and ∠W, ∠U and ∠X; 3. ∠V and ∠X, ∠U and ∠W; 4. ∠T and ∠X, ∠V and ∠Z, ∠S and ∠W, ∠U and ∠Y; 5. ∠U and ∠T, ∠S and ∠V, ∠X and ∠Y, ∠W and ∠Z; 6. ∠S and ∠U, ∠X and ∠Z, ∠T and ∠V, ∠W and ∠Y; 7. corresponding; 8. alternate exterior; 9. alternate interior; 10. consecutive interior; 11. alternate exterior; 12. corresponding; 13. outlet; 14. gift; 15. bracelet; 16. minutes; 17. life; 18. roses; 19. Miss Osbourne; 20. career; 21. B; 22. A; 23. C; 24. C; 25. A; 26. B; Beki: jersey number 34, 10 minutes; Joey: jersey number 13, 11 minutes; Nick: jersey number 20, 12 minutes; Carmen: jersey number 2, 14 minutes

Day 8/Page 17: 1. 214 times; 2. 21 times; 3. 31 times; 4. class; 5. them; 6. you; 7. me; 8. us; 9. him; 10. her; 11. Miss Sherman; 12. volunteers; 13. brother; 14.–21. Answers will vary but may include: 14. drew a line in the sand, created a boundary; 15. keep your shirt on, stay calm; 16. went belly up, died; 17. keep a straight face, not show emotion; 18. in a dead heat, in a tie; 19. a bull in a china shop, clumsily breaking things; 20. wade through the stack, sort through; 21. jockeyed for position, tried to be first in line.

Day 9/Page 19:

white						rye						pumpernickel					
ham		turkey		tofu		ham		turkey		tofu		ham		turkey		tofu	
s c p	s c p	s c p	s c p	s c p	s c p	s c p	s c p	s c p

There are 27 possible outcomes.; 1.–4. Answers will vary; 5. Answers will vary but may include: describing life and landscapes; *fields, brook, autumn eve, trees, moon*; 6. They enjoy doing it.; 7. the moon; 8. It makes each stanza seem like an episode in a story or a scene in a movie.

Day 10/Page 21: 1. $\frac{1}{6}$; 2. $\frac{7}{18}$; 3. $\frac{4}{9}$; 4. $\frac{5}{9}$; 5. $\frac{5}{9}$; 6. $\frac{5}{9}$; 7. Anna, a great actress, got the lead role in the play.; 8. The United Nations, an influential international organization, is based in New York City.; 9. Bridget and Connor, both geologists, work at the Field Museum in Chicago, Illinois.; 10.–19. Answers will vary, but may include: 10. unwieldy; 11. exhausted; 12. scornful; 13. affluence; 14. pointless; 15. balance; 16. overthrow; 17. memorialize; 18. hairy; 19. overused

Day 11/Page 23: 1. 47.1 cm; 2. 18.84 yd.; 3. 40.82 ft.; 4. 6.28 m; 5. 2,122.64 m²; 6. 706.5 ft.²; 7. 1,133.54 yd.²; 8. 176.625 mm²; 9. I, **everyone**; 10. P, **You**; 11. P, **He**; 12. P, **them**; 13. P, **It**; 14. P, **you**; 15. I, **Neither**; 16. P, **They**; 17. D, **These**; 18. P, **I**; 19. D, **That**; 20. I, **Many**; 21. D, **This**; 22. I, **anybody**; 23. Internet; 24. atlas; 25. almanac; 26. newspaper or magazine; 27. encyclopedia; 28. nonfiction books; 29. B; 30. F; 31. H; 32. J; 33. A; 34. D; 35. E; 36. G; 37. C; 38. I

Day 12/Page 25: 1. $24.70; 2. 33%; 3. $1.54; 4. $23,655.91; 5. R; 6. I; 7. I; 8. R; 9. R; 10. I; 11. R; 12. I; 13. R; 14. R; 15. F; 16. T; 17. T; 18. F; 19. T; 20. F; 21. F; Students' writing will vary.

Day 13/Page 27: 1. 60; 2. 36; 3. -9; 4. 74; 5. -36; 6. $\frac{1}{3}$; 7. scalene; 8. acute; 9. obtuse; 10. isosceles; 11. right; 12.–13. Students should draw triangles as described.; 14. C; 15. C; 16. the ballroom at night.

Day 14/Page 29: 1. 0; 2. 39; 3. 472; 4. 22; 5. -91; 6. -143; 7. -23; 8. -7; 9. 53; 10. -17; 11. -13; 12. 5; 13. 13; 14. 15; 15. 9; 16. -25. Students should circle the words in green: 16. N, **we**; 17. N, **She**; 18. O, **him**; 19. N, **They**; 20. O, **me**; 21. O, **her**; 22. N, **They**; 23. O, **him**; 24. O, **them**; 25. O, **me** 26. amphibians and reptiles; 27. Answers will vary.; Students' writing will vary.

Day 15/Page 31: 1. 25; 2. -2; 3. 120; 4. -289; 5. 102; 6. 93; 7. -666; 8. 54; 9. -15; 10. -$\frac{35}{6}$; 11. -106; 12.

145
© Carson Dellosa Education

52; 13. -4; 14. -40; 15. -20; 16. -$\frac{29}{8}$; Stepping off the plane, Mrs. Jackson arrived in Costa Rica at noon. As soon as **she** got to her hotel, **she** enjoyed a light lunch at the restaurant. After lunch, Mr. Jackson, who had taken a different flight, joined **her**. "Let's go to the beach," **he** said. **They** changed into swimsuits, and off **they** went. That evening, **they** called **their** son, Max. "**We** are having a great time," **they** told **him**.; 17. drama; 18. fable; 19. fantasy; 20. Folklore; 21. Horror; 22. legend

Day 16/Page 33: 1. 260 calories per hour, 294 calories per hour, Nelson; 2. 5.25 minutes per mile, 4.5 minutes per mile, Kelsha; 3. $4.67 per pound, $4.15 per pound, Nicholas; 4. to become weaker or end; 5. rebuked, sternly criticized; 6. self-possessed, assured; 7. very upset, agitated; 8. sharp, harsh, unpleasant; 9. B; 10. igneous, sedimentary, metamorphic; 11. Volcanic rock releases magma, which then cools.; 12. Water deposits sediment, which compresses into layers over time.; 13. They begin as igneous or sedimentary rocks. Then, they are squeezed within Earth's crust.

Day 17/Page 35: 1. 1.25; 2. 0.4167; 3. 0.7; 4. 0.$\overline{66}$; 5. 0.33; 6. 0.875; 7. D; 8. I; 9. I; 10. D; 11.–19. Students should circle the words in green: 11. **I want to be the first to volunteer** whenever the teacher asks for help.; 12. If you stay until the birthday party is over, **call Mom for a ride home.**; 13. When monsoon season begins, **the humidity makes the air uncomfortable.**; 14. **Pizza is Crawford's choice for dinner,** but only if it has a thin crust.; 15. We stopped playing and sought shelter **when the storm began.**; 16. **Gabe hopped off his skateboard so that his friend could use it.**; 17. **We won the state championship because we played together as a team.**; 18. **Although the price of gasoline rose by 50 cents per gallon,** Americans did not curb their travel plans.; 19. **If we fail to finish our project tonight,** we will not be in Mrs. Hooper's good graces tomorrow.; 20. mystery; 21. myth; 22. poetry; 23. biography; 24. essay; 25. goods; 26. services; 27. demand; 28. natural resources; 29. inflation; 30. capital resources; 31. supply; 32. scarcity

Day 18/Page 37: 1. $3x + 9$; 2. $5y - 1$; 3. $-2a - 1$; 4. $-x - 3$; 5. $7y - 3$; 6. $5b - 1$; 7. $8(2y - 1)$; 8. $9x(2x - 1)$; 9. $-4(3c + 2)$; 10. S; 11. C; 12. S; 13. C; 14. C; 15. S; 16. C; 17. S; 18. C; 19. S; 20. 90°, complementary; 21. A, supplementary; 22. 45°, 135°, 45°; 23. 180°; 24. 90°; 25. complementary; 26. cilia; 27. macronucleus; 28. food vacuole; 29. cytoplasm; 30. anal pore; 31. oral groove; 32. micronucleus; 33. cell membrane

Day 19/Page 39: 1. 72.5; 2. -1$\frac{13}{27}$; 3. $\frac{-55}{189}$; 4. 2$\frac{3}{5}$; 5. 4.35; 6. $\frac{-3}{49}$; 7. -8.1; 8. -30.4 or -30$\frac{2}{5}$; 9. $\frac{20}{21}$; 10. $\frac{18}{25}$; 11. -3.564; 12. $\frac{4}{3}$ or 1$\frac{1}{3}$; 13. forgot, forgotten; 14. taught, taught; 15. sank, sunk; 16. broke, broken; 17. froze, frozen; 18. threw, thrown; 19. chose, chosen; 20. heard, heard; 21. C; 22. C; 23. because of its alleged magical powers; 24. Answers will vary.

Day 20/Page 41: 1. equation: $6[18 + (18 \div 2) + (18 \times 1\frac{1}{2})] = x$, answer: $324; 2. equation: $(14 \times 2) + 6x = 76$, answer: $8; 3. Oliver Twist, the main character from the Charles Dickens novel Oliver Twist, a poor orphan who asks for more to eat at an orphanage; 4. Alice falling down the rabbit hole, the main character Alice from the Lewis Carroll novel Alice's Adventures in Wonderland who has adventures after she falls into a rabbit hole; 5. build an ark, Noah, a character from the Bible who builds an ark to escape a great flood; 6. Achilles' heel, the warrior Achilles from Greek mythology who was invulnerable in every part of his body except his heel; 7. Cinderella, the poor, overworked main character from the fairy tale "Cinderella"; 8. Scrooge, character Ebenezer Scrooge from the Charles Dickens novel A Christmas Carol who is cold-hearted and greedy; Answers will vary but may include: the perfect pet for everyone, fantastic addition to every home, all turtles are lazy, dogs or cats are cute and frisky, turtles are sluggish but still fascinating, you will have to purchase; Students' writing will vary.

Bonus Page 44: 1.–4. Answers will vary.; 5. ways that animals change over time to help them survive in an environment

Bonus Page 45: 1. Hong Kong; 2. London; 3. Atlanta; 4. Edinburgh; 5. New Delhi; 6. Johannesburg; 7. Barcelona; 8. Calgary; 9. San Francisco; 10. São Paulo; 11. 49°N, 2°E; 12. 49°N, 123°W; 13. 40°N, 116°E; 14. 38°N, 24°E; 15. 12°S, 77°W; 16. 42°N, 71°W; 17. 21°N, 158°W; 18. 19°N, 99°W; 19. 45°N, 12°E; 20. 56°N, 37°E

Bonus Page 46: Answers will vary.

Bonus Page 47: Design and items on time lines will vary.

Section II

Day 1/Page 51: 1. -5; 2. $28y$; 3. $-18x + 15y - 12xy$; 4. $9x + 21y$; 5. $x + 5y + 5$; 6. $3x^2 - 2y^2 + 6x + 9y^2$; 7. $-7x + 20y$; 8. $-6c + 4d$; 9. $-4a - 26b$; 10. $-x - 2y$; 11. $25x + 90y$; 12. $-18x - 12y$; 13. $27x - 9y$; 14. $-6a - 16b + 24z$; 15. $-23x$; 16. $-6y^2 + 3y - 6x - 9$; 17. While I was studying for a history test, Dad called me down for dinner.; 18. When I was practicing piano after dinner, my sister said I was really improving.; 19. While we were walking the trail at the park, the birds sang cheerfully.; 20. After listening to me rehearse my lines for the play, Mom said she thought I'd do very well on opening night.; 21. Though Darren was not very athletic, he taught Micah to play football.; 22. N; 23. P; 24. P; 25. P; 26. P; 27. N; 28. N; 29. N; 30. translucent; 31. opaque; 32. diffuse reflection; 33. ray; 34. reflection; 35. convex; 36. lens; 37. transparent; 38. focal point; 39. concave

Day 2/Page 53: 1. 3; 2. t; 3. $4(12) + 4(15)$; 4. $3(a + 2b)$; 5. $10t + 13t$; 6. $6x + 8x$; 7. $r(7 + 8) + 2$; 8. $2(5x) + 2(8y)$ or $10x + 16y$; 9. $8a + 15$; 10. $4k + 12$; 11. $10b + 8$; 12. $17c + 27$; 13.–19. Students should circle the words in orange: 13. present progressive, **is running**; 14. past progressive, **was staying**; 15. past perfect; **had told**; 16. future progressive, **will be approving**; 17. present perfect, **have played**; 18. past progressive, **were swaying**; 19. future progressive, **will be interviewing**; 20. A; 21. a network of trade routes leading from Asia to the West; 22. goods such as gold, silver, silk, and spices; 23. It was several thousand miles long and was considered dangerous.; 24. the magnetic compass

Day 3/Page 55: 1. $x = 12$; 2. $t = 3$; 3. $m = -6$; 4. $k = 7$; 5. $s = 6$; 6. $r = -96$; 7. $d = 29$; 8. $h = -150$; 9. $c = 8$; 10. $j = -38$; 11. $p = 0$; 12. $z = 7$; 13. melancholy, depressed; 14. introverted, sociable; 15. placate, appease; 16. compulsory, voluntary; 17. response, stimulus; 18. valid, legitimate; 19. cultivate, neglect; 20. A; 21. B; 22. A; 23. A; 24. B; 25. 12; 26. -10; 27. 0; 28. 25; 29. 9; 30. -15

Day 4/Page 57: Students' writing will vary.; 1.–4. Students should circle the words in orange: 1. Even though they were exhausted from their long day, the seventh graders held a dance that night, and the eighth graders saw a play.; 2. Isaac Newton described the relationship between force, mass, and acceleration, and he made discoveries in optics and mathematics, to name just a few of his contributions to science.; 3. Nikki has learned some computer coding, but she also wants to study graphic design, which is being taught at the community center this winter.; 4. After a huge victory last week, the Jayhawks are a favorite in today's game, so a trip to the playoffs could be in their future.; measure; view; build; speak; stars; space; large, powerful; time; little, tiny; angle

Day 5/Page 59: 1. A = 64 m², P = 32 m; 2. A = 70 mm², P = 38 mm; 3. A = 24 yd.², P = 24 yd.; 4. A = 120 m², P = 52 m; 5. A = 100 yd.², P = 64 yd.; 6. A = 52 m², P = 36 m; 7.–14. Students should circle the words in orange: 7. Kiley, brings; 8. Gretchen, goes; 9. Carlos, Ben, have been; 10. statue, stands; 11. teams, call; 12. Trail Ridge Road, winds; 13. questions, were; 14. president, vice president, run; 15. A; 16. C; 17. to explain how Robinson was a pioneer of racial integration in professional sports, The author supports this idea by explaining how Robinson stayed on the Dodgers even though many did not want him to.; 18. He made it possible for people of all races to participate in sports.

Day 6/Page 61: 1. 420 m³; 2. 512 ft.³; 3. 256 cm³; 4. 300 yd.³; 5. 122.5 ft.³; 6. 83.33 mm³; 7. B, dwindle; 8. B, forfeit; 9. C, asterisk; 10. B, rigorous; 11. C, acquaint; 12. A, dismal; 13. A, centennial; 14. B, analogy; 15. C, redundant; 16. A, austere; 17. A, efficient; 18. C, capacity; 19. C; 20. B; 21. B; 22. A; 23. D; 24. D; 25. C; 26. A; Students' writing will vary.

Day 7/Page 63: 1. $x = 2$; 2. $d = 7\frac{1}{2}$; 3. $l = 16$; 4. $m = 33\frac{1}{3}$; 5. $n = 1$; 6. $t = 9$; 7. $v = 1.4$; 8. $z = 3\frac{1}{5}$; 9. $s = 36$; 10. $c = 24$; 11. $r = 3$; 12. $b = 18$; 13. $k = 3$; 14. $w = 4$; 15. $f = 4$; 16. $h = 16\frac{2}{3}$;

17.
18.
19.
20.

Possible answer: The mean of Homeroom A is 6 books, and the mean of Homeroom B is 7 books. Therefore, Homeroom B read on average more books than Homeroom A.; 21. key, ring; 22. ring, finger; 23. finger, snap; 24. snap, dragon; 25. dragon, fly; 26. fly, ball; 27. ball, game

Day 8/Page 65: 1. $8.75; 2. 18 ounces; 3. $12.50; 4. $1.76; 5. $9.15; 6. $42.88; 7.–9. Answers will vary but may include: 7. Kelly worked for years as a consultant for Harnquist and Beckman and now has her own consulting firm.; 8. Lake Powell, which occupies parts of both Arizona and Utah, is the largest lake in either state.; 9. We had box seats in the front row, so we could put our drinks on top of the Cardinal's dugout.; 10. They support a dazzling array of life.; 11. B; 12. rain forests; 13. to form limestone to support their soft bodies; 14. The author thinks that coral reefs are amazing and fragile wonders of nature.; 15. Coral may appear permanent, but is actually easily damaged.

Day 9/Page 67: 1. 50%; 2. 19%; 3. 45; 4. 20; 5. 15.32; 6. .84; 7. 25%; 8. .90; 9. 38.88; 10. 58%; 11. A; 12. P; 13. A; 14. P; 15. P; 16. P; 17. A; 18. P; 19. P; 20. P; 21. B; 22. D; 23. F; 24. A; 25. G; 26. E; 27. C; 28. H

Day 10/Page 69: 1. $A = 6$ yd.², $P = 12$ yd.; 2. $A = 35$ m², $P = 34$ m; 3. 45 in.², $P = 34$ in.; 4. $A = 73.5$ ft.², $P = 46$ ft.; 5. $A = 67.5$ cm², $P = 45$ cm; 6. $A = 150$ yd.², $P = 55$ yd.; 7. $A = 21$ m², $P = 27$ m; 8. $A = 54$ cm², $P = 36$ cm; 9. $A = 67.5$ ft.², $P = 39$ ft.; 10. twisting, PR; 11. covered, PA; 12. trampled, PA; 13. jumping, PR; 14. broken, PA; 15. C; 16. F; 17. A; 18. H; 19. D; 20. E; 21. B; 22. G; 23. outer core; 24. crust; 25. mantle; 26. lithosphere; 27. inner core; 28. atmosphere

Day 11/Page 71: 1. R; 2. R; 3. R; 4. R; 5. R; 6. R; 7. I; 8. R; 9. I; 10. I; 11. R; 12. R; 13. A; 14. J; 15. D; 16. G; 17. B; 18. H; 19. F; 20. I; 21. C; 22. E; 23.–25. Answers will vary. Possible answers: 23. Molly is courageous. She is quick to act, and she manages to keep calm and steady, even in times of crisis.; 24. During the Revolutionary War, a woman named Molly Pitcher brought water to soldiers in battle and operated a cannon in a time of crisis.; 25. The facts of the story would be the same, but William would have a different perspective as a soldier. He would also be likely to feel both proud of Molly and worried for her safety.

Day 12/Page 73: 1. G; 2. H; 3. C; 4. E; 5. D; 6. J; 7. I; 8. L; 9. B; 10. F; 11. K; 12. A; 13. ADV; 14. ADJ; 15. ADJ; 16. ADV; 17. ADV; 18. ADV; 19. ADV; 20. Answers will vary but may include: Getting sufficient sleep is essential to repair the body and fight sickness.; 21. Answers will vary.; 22. to give useful information about how to get a good night's sleep for improved health; 23. Yes, the author gives lots of facts and examples about the importance of sleep.

Day 13/Page 75: 1. $6^1 = 6$; 2. $2^6 = 64$; 3. $5^3 = 125$; 4. $3^5 = 243$; 5. $7^{-1} = \frac{1}{7}$; 6. $10^3 = 1,000$; 7. $10^8 = 100,000,000$; 8. $6^1 = 6$; 9. $4^3 = 64$; 10. $8^4 = 4,096$; 11. $11^{-2} = \frac{1}{121}$; 12. $2^{-6} = \frac{1}{64}$; 13. The movie <u>The Sound of Music</u> fascinated me.; 14. The deputy's words amazed the young children in the classroom.; 15. Meghan's cat Buffy chased the toy.; 16. When Lucy opened the soft drink, it sprayed her in the face.; 17. Andy Rahal scored a goal for the Crosby Middle School soccer team.; Answers will vary.

Day 14/Page 77:

1.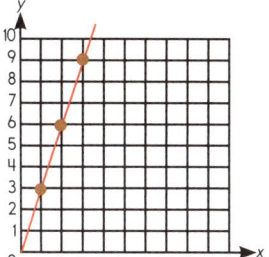

2.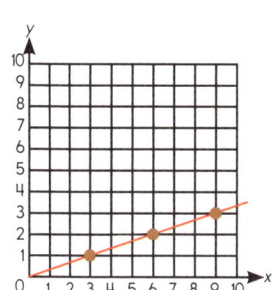

3.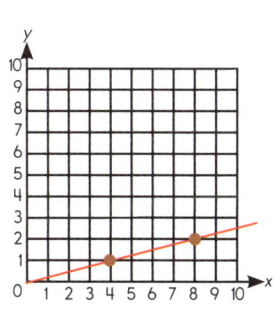

4.

5.–13. Students should circle the words in orange: 5. <u>by the phone</u>, <u>in the Louisville, Kentucky, airport</u>; 6. <u>with the city</u>; 7. <u>without that information</u>; 8. <u>in</u> the tree; 9. <u>to the movies</u>; 10. <u>to the booth</u>, <u>of the new broadcast team</u>; 11. <u>under the cushions</u>, <u>of the sofa</u>; 12. <u>under</u> the two buildings; 13. <u>at Italian restaurants</u>; 14. B; 15. beautiful mountains, glaciers, Lake Louise, wildlife; 16. Animals reproduce rapidly.; It is hard to control misuse.; Animals are targets for poachers.; 17. geysers, hot springs, scenery; 18. C; 19. to explain factors that make it difficult to protect environments in national parks; Yes, the author accomplishes this purpose by providing several examples.

Day 15/Page 79: 1. 13; 2. 100; 3. 9; 4. 4; 5. 8; 6. 25; 7. 12; 8. 15; 9. 20; 10. 6; 11. 30; 12. 50; 13.–22. Conjunctions will vary but may include: 13. or; 14. and; 15. but; 16. but; 17. and; 18. but; 19. and; 20. but; 21. and; 22. and; 23. B; 24. E; 25. I; 26. A; 27. H; 28. C; 29. D; 30. F; 31. G; 32. granite; 33. limestone; 34. slate; 35. marble

Day 16/Page 81: 1. $c = 13$ m; 2. $c = 12.04$ cm; 3. $c = 7.07$ yd.; 4. $b = 4.90$ ft.; 5. $b = 5.20$ mm; 6. $a = 8$ in.; 7. $b = 2.24$ ft.; 8. $a = 3$ cm; 9. B; 10. A; 11. A; 12. C; 13. B; 14. A; 15. B; 16. C; Mrs. Jackson was unable to buy a new watch.; Answers will vary but may include: "You only have $25 in your account."; 17. B; 18. F; 19. B; 20. A; 21. F; 22. D; 23. A; 24. C; 25. E; 26. E

Day 17/Page 83: 1. yes; 2. yes; 3. no; 4. yes; 5. no; 6. yes; 7.–14. Answers will vary but may include: 7. both, and; 8. both, and; 9. either, or; 10. neither, nor; 11. Both, and; 12. whether, or; 13. both, and; 14. Either, or; 15. C; 16. 3, 2, 5,1, 4; 17. C; 18. Farmers and ranchers dislike mustangs because the animals destroy crops and interfere with livestock.

Day 18/Page 85: 1. 1,004.8 ft.³; 2. 280 mm³; 3. 80 cm³; 4. 216 m³; 5. 75.40 yd.³; 6. 268.08 m³; 7.–12.

Answers will vary.; 13. T; 14. T; 15. T; 16. P; 17. T; 18. T; 19. T; 20. T; 21. P; 22. P; 23. T; 24. P; 25. P; 26. P; 27.–28. Answers will vary.; 29. gravity; 30. speed; 31. velocity; 32. weight; 33. friction; 34. force; 35. momentum; 36. inertia; 37. acceleration; 38. mass

Day 19/Page 87: 1. acute, equilateral; 2. right, scalene; 3. obtuse, scalene; 4. acute, equilateral; 5. acute, scalene; 6. acute, equilateral; 7. right, isosceles; 8. acute, isosceles; 9. right, scalene; Check students' work.; 10. weight and miles per gallon; 11. negative, The line of best fit slopes downward.; 12. D; 13. D; 14. C; 15. D; 16. C; 17. A; Students' writing will vary.

Day 20/Page 89: 1. $x = 25$; 2. $y = 240$; 3. $w = 8$; 4. $a = -24$; 5. $r = 343$; 6. $m = -6$; 7. $b = 12$; 8. $x = 18$; 9. $k = -24$; 10. $c = -14$; 11. $x = 369$; 12. $y = 180$; 13.–18. Students should circle the words in orange: 13. knowing, know; 14. hearing, hear; 15. floating, float; 16. complaining, complain; 17. putting, putt; 18. going, go; 19. To snowboard; 20. to do; 21. to play; 22. to attempt; 23. to study; 24.–29. Answers will vary but may include: 24. Indian and South Pacific Oceans; 25. It has two rows of 80 to 100 tentacles that surround its head.; It has an external shell with many chambers; 26. shrimp, fish, molted shell chambers; 27. They attach to rocks, coral, or the seafloor.; 28. has arms; 29. cannot change color or squirt ink

Bonus Page 91: Answers will vary.

Bonus Page 93: 1. California; 2. Alberta; 3. the Atlantic Ocean; 4. Georgia; 5. New Mexico; 6. the Arctic Ocean; 7. the Sierra Nevada Mountains; 8. 40°N; 9. 60°N; 10. 40°N, 90°W; 11. 90°W

Bonus Page 94: 1. E; 2. G; 3. B; 4. I; 5. C; 6. F; 7. D; 8. H; 9. A; Answers will vary.

Bonus Page 95: 1. Grand Canyon; 2. Taj Mahal; 3. Parthenon; 4. Easter Island; 5. Great Wall of China; 6. Sydney Opera House; 7. Leaning Tower of Pisa; 8. Stonehenge; 9. Sphinx; 10. Mount Rushmore

Section III

Day 1/Page 99: 78°; 2. 5 mm; 3. 60°; 4. 67°; 5. 70°; 6. 61°; 7. Four score and seven years ago our fathers brought forth…a new nation…dedicated to the proposition that all men are created equal.; 8. Now we are engaged in a great civil war, testing whether that nation…can long endure.; 9. But, in a larger sense, we cannot dedicate…this ground.; 10. Prefix: ex-, Root Word: press, Suffix: -ible; 11. Prefix: un-, Root Word: believe, Suffix: -able; 12. Root Word: drama, Suffix: -tize; 13. Root Word: allow, Suffix: -ance; 14. Prefix: re-, Root Word: search, Suffix: -er; 15. B. 139.20 rubles, 104.20 rubles, $0.83; C. 274.75 yen, $1.51; D. $1.63, $3.37

Day 2/Page 101: 1. 10.6; 2. 76.3; 3. 3 and 4; 4. 4 and 5; 5. 6 and 7; 6. 2 and 3; 7. 1 and 2; 8. 4 and 5; 9. $\sqrt{18}$, 4π, 14; 10. 2, $\sqrt{5}$, 5; 11. D; 12. C; 13. C; 14. D; 15. A; 16. B; Students' writing will vary.

Day 3/Page 103: 1. 2.5×10^5; 2. 1.2×10^{-4}; 3. 3.65×10^6; 4. 4.5×10^{10}; 5. 9.6×10^{-5}; 6. 1.23×10^5; 7. 320,000; 8. 0.000000641; 9. 1,200,000,000; 10. 7,040; 11. 0.00000114; 12. 10,900,000; 13. I; 14. IN; 15. IM; 16. C; 17. IN; 18. IM; 19. I; 20. C; 21. I; 22. IN; 23. C; 24. B; 25. Answers will vary.; 26. a smaller representative group; 27. by asking a subsample the question

Day 4/Page 105:

1. (4, 8)

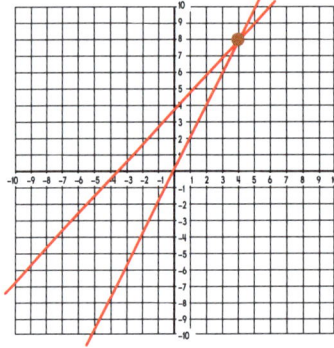

2. (3, 4)

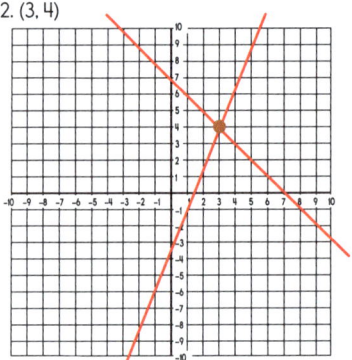

3. My aunt–she lives just a few miles away–has a horse and six chickens.; 4. Enrique texted his best friend–he just got a new phone–to see what Colin's plans were for the weekend.; 5. After you've mixed in the mashed bananas–make sure you've sprayed the pan with cooking spray–you can carefully scrape the batter into the pan.; 6. H; 7. A; 8. I; 9. G; 10. D; 11. E; 12. F; 13. B; 14. C

Day 5/Page 107: 1. $y = \frac{1}{3}x - 6$; 2. $y = 2x + 5$; 3. $y = \frac{3}{2}x + 4$; 4. $y = 7x - 5$; 5. $y = -2x - 3$; 6.–9. Answers will vary.; 10.–16. Rephrased answers will vary but circled words include: 10. very cool; 11. don't get it; 12. props; 13. What's up?; 14. in; 15. chill; 16. hit it out of the park; 17. C; 18. B; 19. E; 20. F; 21. G; 22. A; 23. D

Day 6/Page 109: 1. 45°; 2. 135°; 3. 50°; 4. 45°; 5. yes, Both triangles share ∠5. ∠8 and ∠16 are corresponding angles, so they have the same measure. ∠11 and ∠19 are also corresponding angles with the same measure. The angles of both triangles are equal measures, so they are similar triangles.; 6. F; 7. F; 8. C; 9. F; 10. F; 11. C; 12. C; 13. Answers will vary.; 14. C; 15. C; 16. A; 17. Answers will vary.

Day 7/Page 111:

1.

x	y
–7	–7
–4	–1
0	7
2	11
5	17

2.

x	y
–10	76
–3	20
1	–12
2	–20
3	–28

3.

x	y
–4	2
–2	3
0	4
8	8
11	$9\frac{1}{2}$

4.

x	y
–6	–29
–1	–14
1	–8
3	–2
5	4

5.

x	y
–16	0
–4	3
0	4
5	$5\frac{1}{4}$
9	$6\frac{1}{4}$

6.

x	y
−40	−55
−23	−38
−16	−31
12	−3
30	15

7.–9. Answers will vary.; Students' conclusions will vary.; 10. E; 11. F; 12. G; 13. D; 14. B; 15. H; 16. C; 17. A

Day 8/Page 113: 1. −5, −1, nonlinear; 2. $\frac{7}{4}$, $\frac{7}{4}$, linear; 3. 2, 18, nonlinear; 4. $\frac{3}{2}$, $\frac{3}{2}$, linear; 5.–12. Answers may vary. Possible answers: 5. stubborn; 6. depressed; 7. spotted, dappled; 8. poisonous, toxic; 9. hatred; 10. outraged; 11. situation; 12. except; 13. immigrated; 14. it's; 15. fare; 16. then; 17. Their; 18. Whose; 19. two; 20. principal; 21. past; 22. that; Stories will vary.

Day 9/Page 115: 1. ∠VUT; ∠UVT; ∠UTV; 2. ∠EDC, ∠FJI; ∠ABC, ∠GHI; ∠BAE, ∠HGF; ∠DEA, ∠JFG; ∠DCB, ∠JIH; 3. ∠EFG; ∠FGH; ∠GHE; ∠HEF; 4. ∠NML, ∠SRQ; ∠JNM, ∠OSR; ∠JKL, ∠OPQ; ∠KLM, ∠PQR; ∠NJK, ∠SOP; 5. ∠MNL, ∠PRQ; ∠MLN, ∠PQR; ∠LMN, ∠QPR; 6. ∠ZWX, ∠BCD; ∠XYZ, ∠DAB; ∠WXY, ∠CDA; ∠YZW, ∠ABC; 7. then; 8. which; 9. Your; 10. that; 11. you're; 12.–14. Answers will vary. Possible answers: 12. The author tells the reader that trouble is brewing. The reader knows that it involves the Arctic and the gold rush, but not what the exact trouble is. This creates suspense and the desire to keep reading.; 13. estate, territory; 14. The story is told from Buck's perspective, which is unusual, because he is a dog.

Day 10/Page 117:

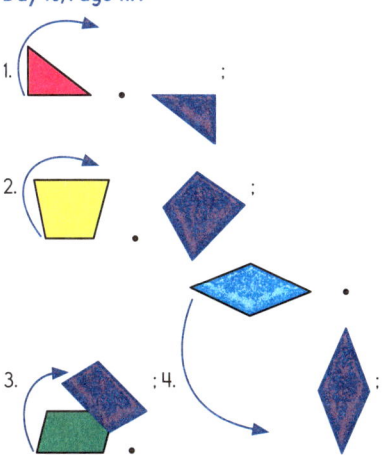

5.–8. Answers will vary but may include: 5. Kelly doesn't want any more interruptions.; 6. Tracie never did anything wrong until she broke her mother's favorite vase.; 7. Dr. Canberra was born in Argentina, but he never traveled anywhere else once he arrived in the United States.; 8. I left home without my umbrella since there is not a chance of rain today.; 9. F; 10. T; 11. T; 12. T; 13. F; 14. F; 15. T; 16. Answers will vary.; 17. ductile; 18. malleable; 19. alloy; 20. reactivity; 21. conductor; 22. magnetic

Day 11/Page 119: 1. yes, reduced; 2. yes, reduced; 3. no, not reduced on equal scale; 4. yes, reduced; 5. no, rotated; 6. yes, expanded; 7. yes, reduced; 8. no, rotated; Students' writing will vary.; B; Underlined details will vary.; 9. C; 10. president and cabinet of advisors; 11. House of Representatives and Senate

Day 12/Page 121: 1. reduction; 2. enlargement; 3. reduction; 4. reduction; 5. enlargement; 6. reduction; 7. enlargement; 8. enlargement; 9. 3:4; 10. 1:3; 11. 3:2; 12. 2:1; 13. When Ana Maria opened her book, she saw a stain on the page.; 14. If I were you, I would have left the performance during intermission.; 15. Pack your lunch, and then let the dog out.; 16. Kiku was elected class president, and she made changes throughout the school year.; 17. If we had won the game, we would have gone out to celebrate afterward.; 18. B; 19. A; 20. 9 miles (15 km); 21. B; 22. the gravitational pull of the planets

Day 13/Page 123: 1. graph; 2. equal; 3. equation; Students should draw three lines under the first letter of the following words: (paragraph 1): Florida, King, Phillip; (paragraph 2): Menendez, Florida, American, Indian, Seloy, American, Indians, St. Augustine.; Order of answers may vary within classifications but will include: I. Animals; A. vertebrates; 1. mammals; a. cows; b. lions; 2. reptiles; a. snakes; b. crocodiles; 3. amphibians; a. salamanders; b. frogs; 4. birds; a. robins; b. cardinals.

Day 14/Page 125: 1. 8, 20, $\frac{4}{15}$; 2. 7, 27, $\frac{7}{30}$; 3. 3, 30, $\frac{1}{10}$; 4. 67–68; 5. 30; 6. 3, 3, $\frac{1}{10}$; 7. 5, 8, $\frac{1}{6}$; 8. 6, 14, $\frac{1}{5}$; 9. 7, 21, $\frac{7}{30}$; 10. 5, 26, $\frac{1}{6}$; 11. 4, 30, $\frac{2}{15}$; 12. 30; 13. 4; 14. N; 15. E; 16. P; 17. nuclear; 18. solar; 19. hydroelectric; 20. wind; 21. geothermal; 22. biomass; 23. gasohol

Day 15/Page 127: 1. 301.44 in.³; 2. 434.67 in.³; 3. 2,884.88 cm³; 4. Glass A holds 64,998 mm³ more liquid than Glass B.; 5.–8. Answers will vary. Possible answers: 5. possible, doable; 6. to place together; 7. having a strong taste; 8. a theme or idea; 9. B; 10. a trace of an ancient animal or plant preserved in Earth's crust; 11. 1990; 12. C; 13. Responses will vary.

Day 16/Page 129: 1. Answers will vary.; 2. 4, 5, 6, 7; 3. 4; 4. low: 46, high: 74; 5. 28; 6. P, The answer, of course, is 44.; 7. A, Bridget, the tallest girl on the team, is a great tennis player.; 8. D, If you wait, Justin, we will go with you.; 9. D, Button, stop scratching the cushions.; 10. D, Nadia, please call your brother on the phone.; 11. D, I told you, Shay, not to wait too long to start your project.; 12. A, Mrs. Ramirez, the hardest seventh-grade English teacher, gave me an A on my essay.; 13.–17. Answers will vary.; 18. physical change; 19. chemical change; 20. physical change; 21. physical change; 22. chemical change

Day 17/Page 131: 1. 8.54; 2. 9.49; 3. 10.44; 4. 9.43; Answers will vary.; 5. glossary; 6. bibliography; 7. index; 8. caption; 9. title page; 10. pictures; 11. table of contents

Day 18/Page 133: 1. (4, 8); 2. (−6, −11); 3. (4, 11); 4. (6, 16); 5. ($\frac{2}{3}$, $\frac{-1}{3}$); 6. (−1$\frac{4}{5}$, 5$\frac{1}{5}$); 7. Mr. Cole decided to meet with Ms. Grayson, Ben's math teacher; Mr. Robbins, his science teacher; and Mrs. Abernathy, his English teacher.; 8. Raymond Webb just graduated from college; he plans to attend law school.; 9. The first rule in this class: respect other students' rights.; 10. The parent company left its main facility open but closed plants in Greensboro, North Carolina; Jacksonville, Florida; and Harrisburg, Pennsylvania.; 11. Will Rogers made this comment on attitude: "Don't let yesterday use up too much of today."; 12. Alyson accepted the job as a telemarketer for one reason: she wanted to work at home while Amy was a baby.; 13. Have you ever heard the quote, "You can't afford the luxury of a negative thought"?; 14. Grace did well in three subjects; therefore, she will have a high average at the end of the semester.; 15. C; 16. theater, dance, sculpting, and painting; 17. They had to pass a difficult exam.; 18. to determine the empire's population; 19. because new roads and canals made travel easier

Day 19/Page 135: 1. >; 2. <; 3. >; 4. >; 5. >; 6. >; 7. <; 8. <; 9. =; The origin of the ice-cream cone has been controversial for several centuries. Some historians claim that the first paper cone came from France, while others maintain that metal cones were used in Germany. Still, other people say that an Italian genius introduced the first ice-cream cone.

Ice cream was referred to in Europe as "iced pudding," and the cones were called "wafers." Eating establishments often served the wafers after a meal to soothe digestion. But, once chefs rolled the wafers into funnels, the cones could be filled with anything, including ice cream.

However, many Americans believe that the first edible ice-cream cone was created in the United States. Italo Marchiony, who emigrated from Italy, created edible cones and sold them from pushcarts in the streets of New York City for a penny each. Marchiony eventually patented his invention in 1903.; 10.–14. Reasons will vary. 10. A; 11. C; 12. D; 13. B; 14. A; Glossaries will vary.

Day 20/Page 137: 1. Equation 1: $q + d = 63$, Equation 2: $25q + 10d = 1,080$, Stella has 30 quarters and 33 dimes.; 2. Equation 1: $a + c = 1,750$, Equation 2: $8a + 3.5c = 9,860$, 830 adults and 920 children attended the event.; 3. B; 4. A; 5. A; 6. A; 7. B; 8. A; 9. B; 10. A;

```
              Ellen (runner)
                 ┌─────┐
Julie (skater)   │     │   Ben (golfer)
                 └─────┘
                  Dante
              (tennis player)
```

11. Johannes Gutenberg; 12. Miguel de Cervantes; 13. Michelangelo; 14. Galileo Galilei; 15. Leonardo da Vinci; 16. John Milton; 17. Nicolaus Copernicus

Bonus Page 139: 1. wind; 2. water; 3. ice

Bonus Page 140: Answers will vary.; orange juice; vinegar; Orange juice; Vinegar

Bonus Page 141: Answers will vary.

Bonus Page 142: Answers will vary but may include Argentina: 41.77 million (est.); Buenos Aires; Spanish; republic; corn, wheat, livestock, petroleum, or other acceptable products; Finland: 5.26 million (est.); Helsinki; Finnish and Swedish; constitutional republic; barley, fish, metals, timber, or other acceptable products; Cambodia: 14.41 million (est.); Phnom Penh; Khmer; democracy under a constitutional monarchy; sugar, rubber, rice, or other acceptable products.

Bonus Page 143: Answers will vary.

evacuate vacuum vacate	incredulous incredible discredit	telescope microscope stethoscope
monogram telegram grammar	conduct educate induct	tractor contract attraction
immobility automobile mobilize	interrupt corruption bankrupt	geography geophysics geology

vid/vis
(see)

derm
(skin)

therm
(heat, warm)

book : library ::
painting : _____

goose : flock ::
wolf : _____

glass : shatter ::
fabric : _____

volcano : lava ::
geyser : _____

flexible : stiff ::
solid : _____

sunny : cheerful ::
sullen : _____

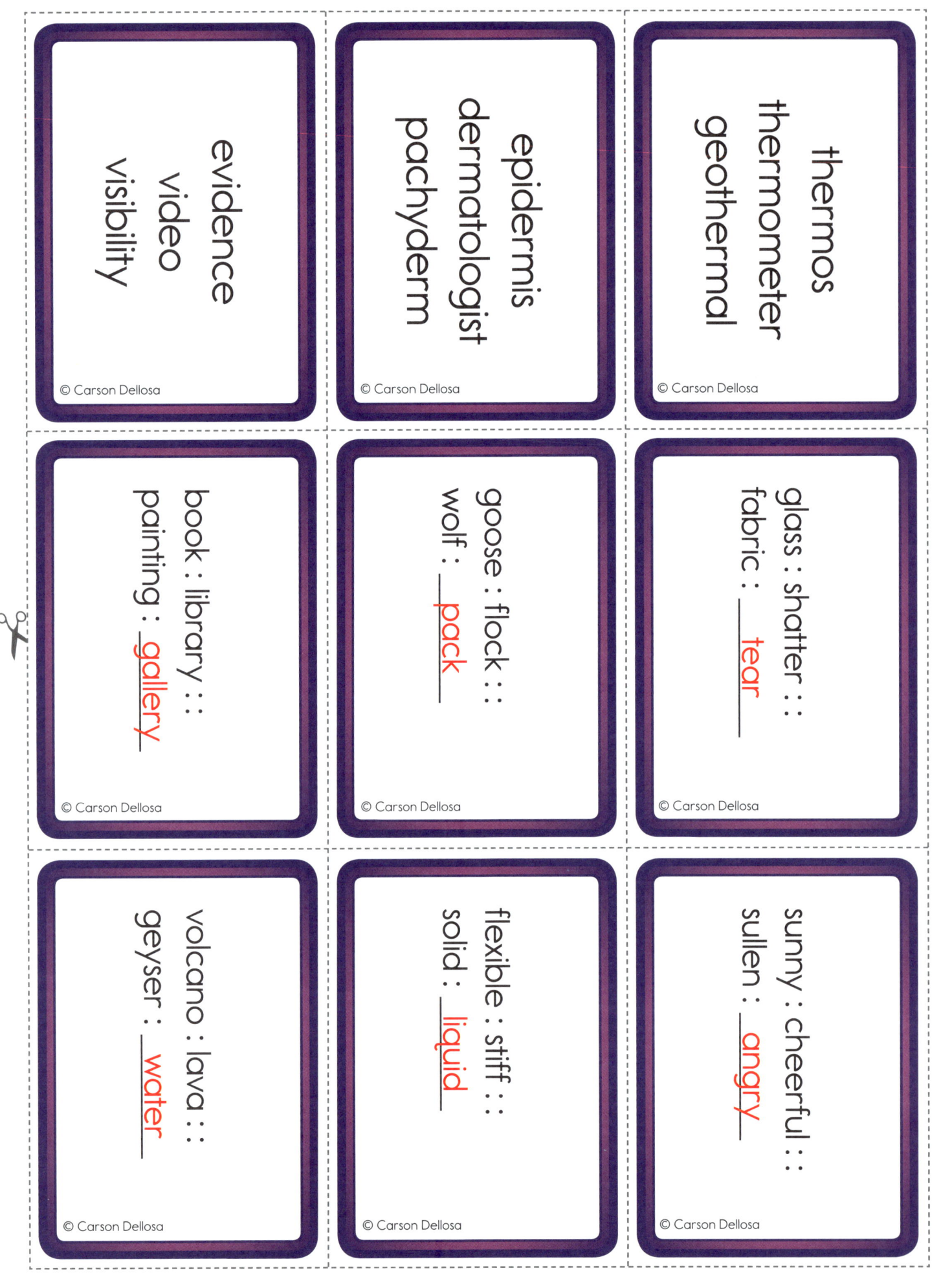

- paper : staple :: wood : ____
- speaker : sound :: flower : ____
- close : clothes :: mind : ____
- raise : construct :: raze : ____
- steeple : church :: mast : ____
- radiate : heat :: illuminate : ____
- sulk : pout :: chortle : ____
- grayed : grade :: warn : ____
- partial : complete :: accelerate : ____

- close : clothes :: mind : __mined__
- speaker : sound :: flower : __smell__
- paper : staple :: wood : __nail__

- radiate : heat :: illuminate : __light__
- steeple : church :: mast : __boat__
- raise : construct :: raze : __destroy__

- partial : complete :: accelerate : __decelerate__
- grayed : grade :: warn : __worn__
- sulk : pout :: chortle : __laugh__

kilometer : distance :: acre : _____	personification	idiom
allusion	irony	pun
$\sqrt{169}$	$\sqrt{49}$	$\sqrt{225}$

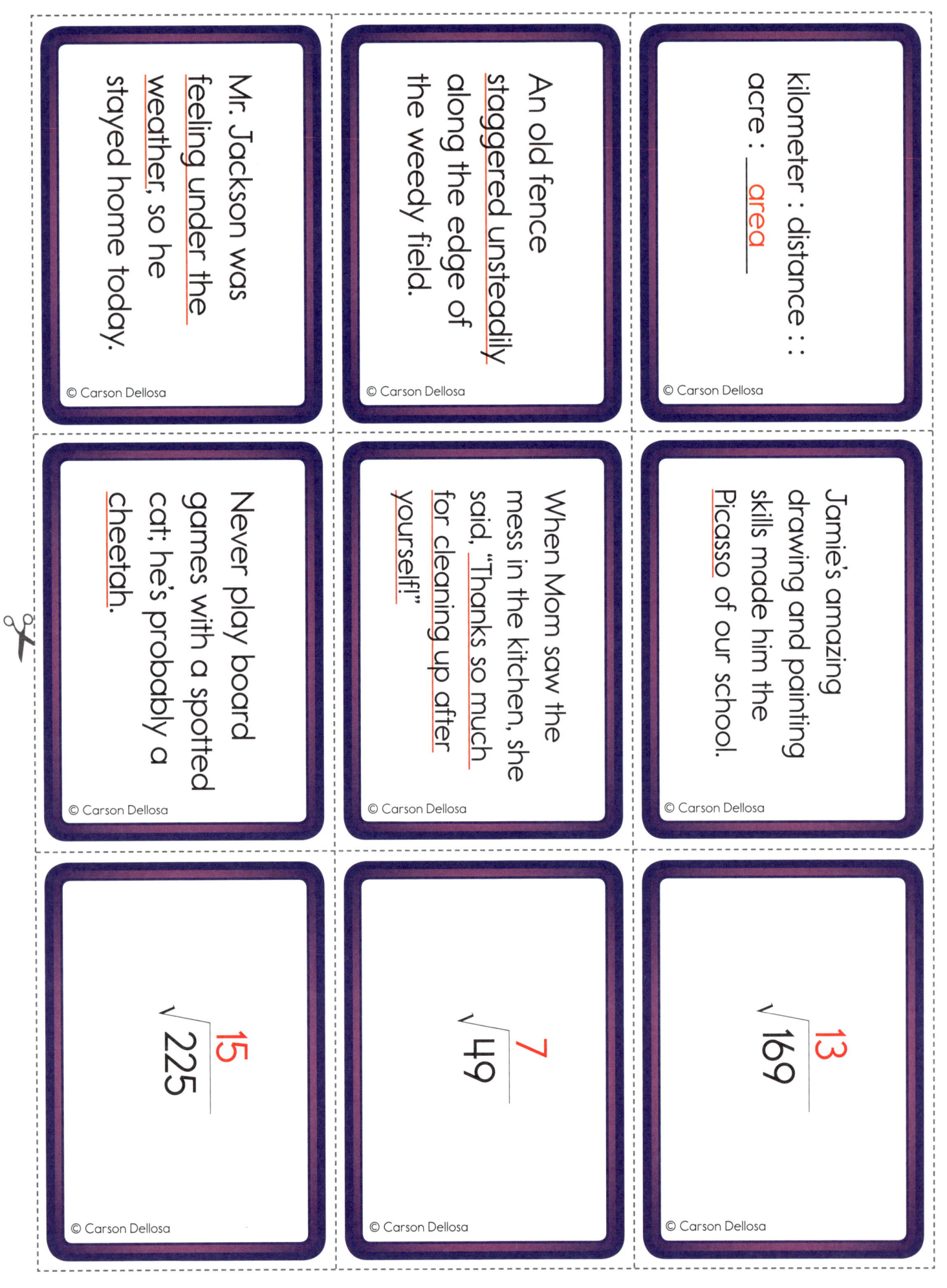

$\sqrt[3]{216}$	$\sqrt[3]{64}$	$\sqrt{400}$
$4.7 \times 10^8 =$ _____	$2.45 \times 10^{-4} =$ _____	$\sqrt[3]{125}$
$320{,}000{,}000 =$ _____ $\times 10$ _____	$5.04 \times 10^5 =$ _____	$8.9 \times 10^{-6} =$ _____

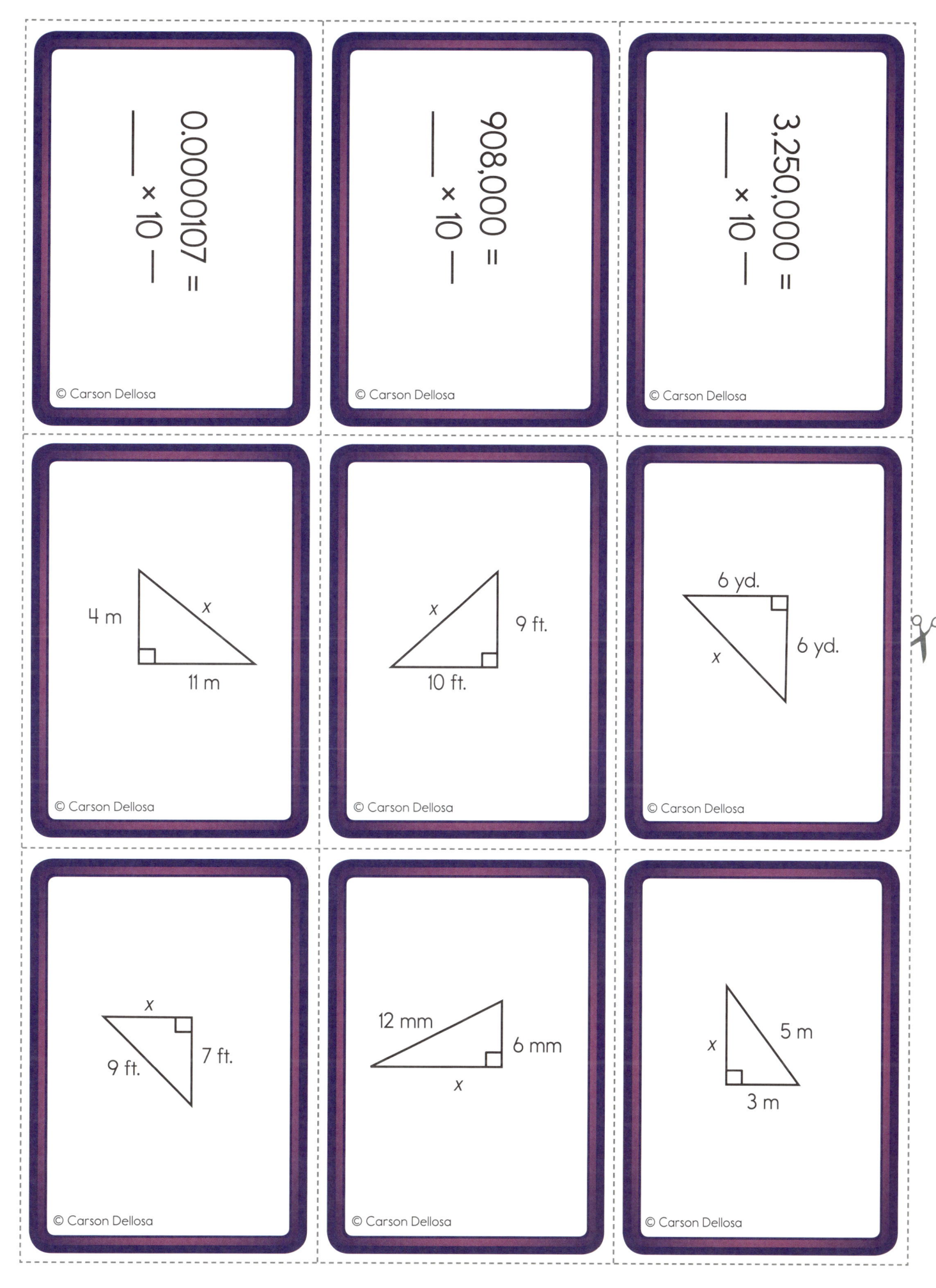

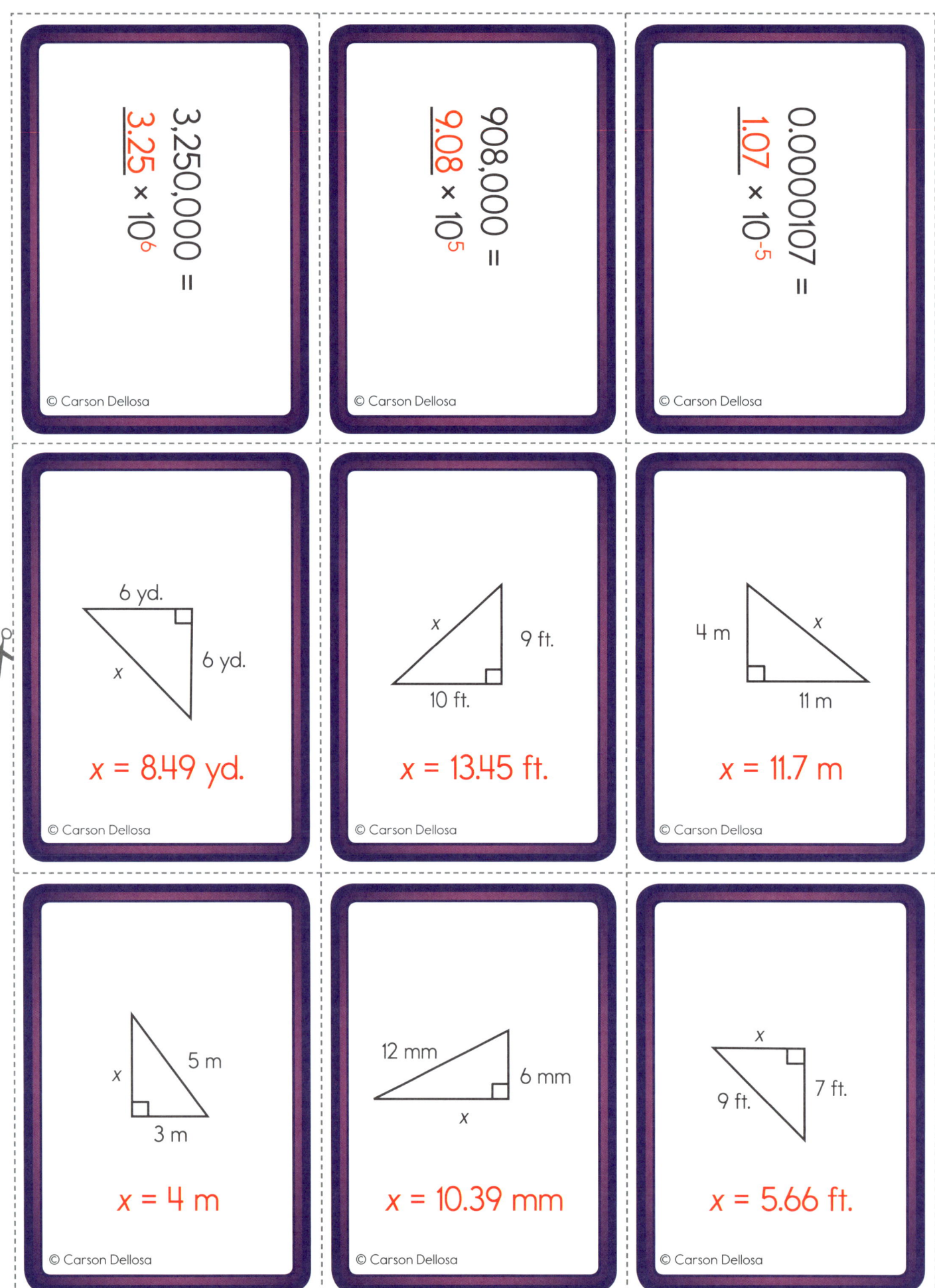

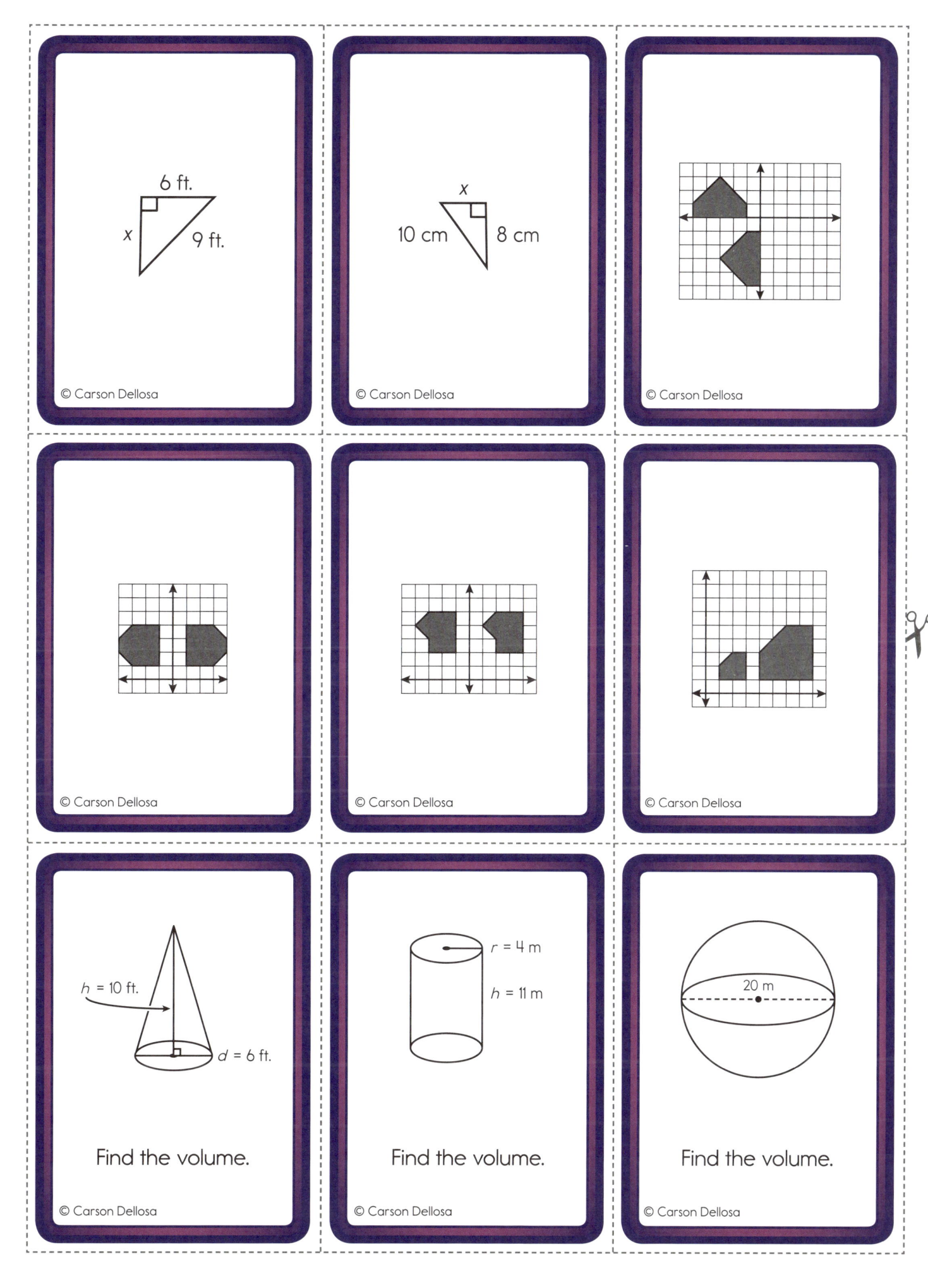

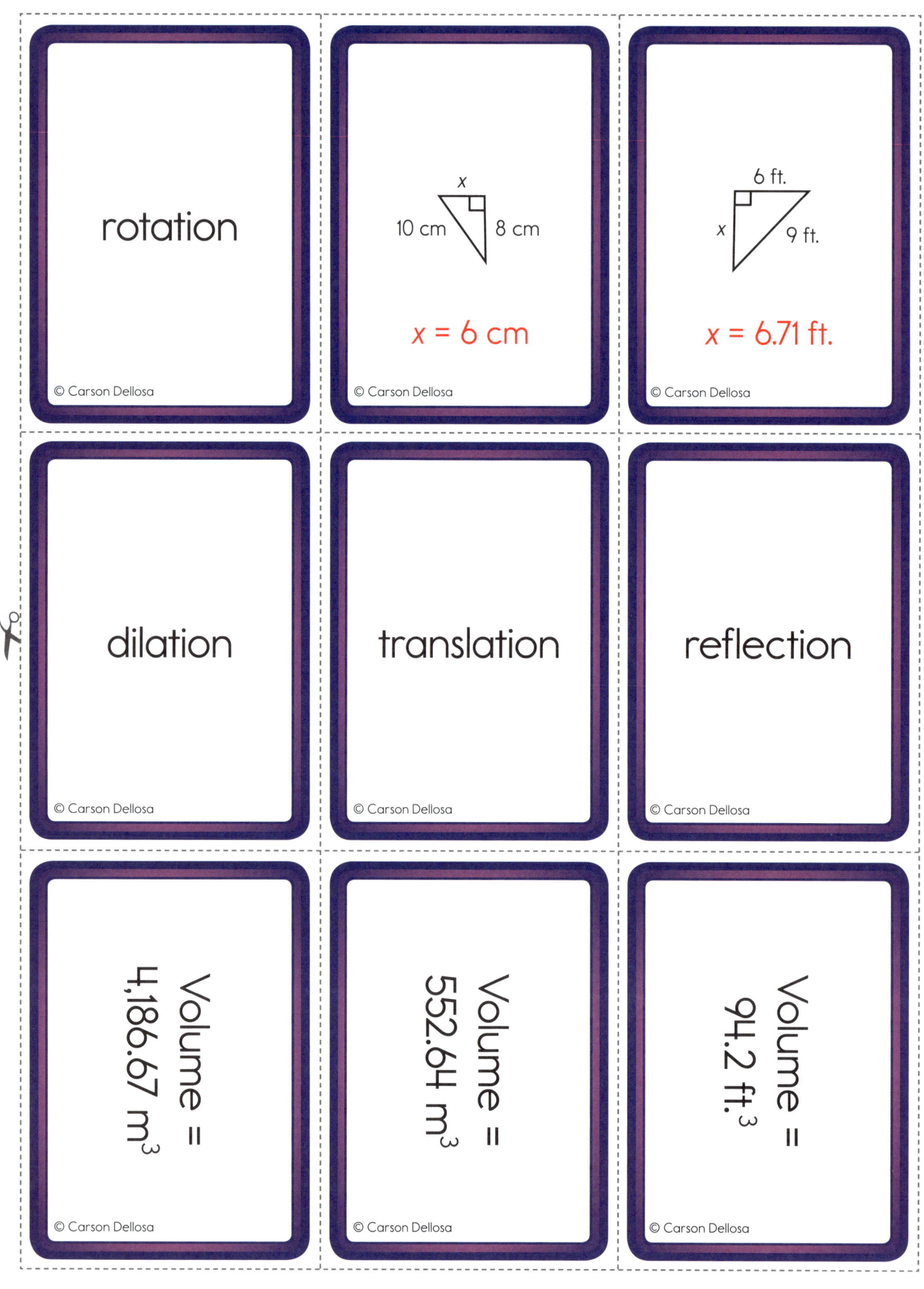